I0540789

My Own Dear Darling Boy

Warbler Press 2021

Oscar Wilde's letters to Lord Alfred Douglas used by permission of Merlin Holland, the Executor of the Estate of Oscar Wilde.

A. S. W. Rosenbach's essay used by permission of The Rosenbach, Philadelphia.

Facsimile of Oscar Wilde's letter to Lord Alfred Douglas courtesy of the Morgan Library and Museum.

Facsimile of Lord Alfred Douglas's letter to Oscar Wilde dated May 15, 1895, courtesy of Rare Book & Manuscript Library, Columbia University in the City of New York.

Preface, Afterword, and Biographical Timeline © 2021 by Ulrich Baer

All rights reserved. No part of this book may be reproduced in any form or by any means, electronic or mechanical, including photocopying, recording, or by any information storage and retrieval system, without permission from the publisher, which may be requested at permissions@warblerpress.com.

ISBN 978-1-954525-67-2 (paperback)
ISBN 978-1-954525-68-9 (e-book)

warblerpress.com

Publisher's Note
Original punctuation has been retained except in a few instances for the sake of clarity, and abbreviations have been lengthened. Obvious spelling errors of names and places have been quietly corrected. The dating of the letters follows the dates established in *The Complete Letters of Oscar Wilde,* edited by Merlin Holland and Rupert Hart-Davis.

My Own Dear Darling Boy

THE LETTERS OF OSCAR WILDE
TO LORD ALFRED DOUGLAS

EDITED AND WITH AN AFTERWORD
BY ULRICH BAER

CONTENTS

PREFACE
by Ulrich Baer

THE WORLD'S GREAT love letters open a window not only on a particular person's innermost feelings, but show us what it means to live our truest self—and give ourselves willingly, joyously, and freely to another. Love letters can be persuasive, pleading, coercive, manipulative, seductive, flattering, charming, and banal. For the recipient, they can reveal the writer on their own terms and, for a brief moment, make them appear present. Love letters can also rise to the level of great literature when their specificity of circumstance and character overflows into the universal, because their language captures a feeling or idea that resonates for all readers. Oscar Wilde's letters to Lord Alfred Douglas contain moments when Wilde's words no longer communicate specific information about himself and his circumstances but appear on the page in a way that lets us glimpse Wilde's mind and heart across time and space and feel something of the startling vibrancy and vitality that infused their love.

The letters gathered here constitute the surviving fraction of approximately one hundred and fifty letters that Bosie destroyed after Wilde's premature death in 1900, at the age of forty-six. But even this partial record articulates a major shift in modern sensibility. Wilde's relationship with Bosie led to several court proceedings which put not only Wilde's homosexuality but also literature and the power of the human imagination itself on trial. Wilde was sentenced to two years of hard labor, while Lord Alfred Douglas fled to France. The ruling turned Wilde into a social pariah in England where he had been rightly celebrated as a major writer. The outcome of the trial also, in time, made Oscar Wilde an icon of gay liberation.

The point of this edition, however, is not to enlist Wilde in a political program or to use the letters as proof of Wilde's love for Bosie, as if the playwright were still on trial today. Rather, it is to let these letters speak across the chasm of time in a way that differs somewhat from the way they have been used in court and in countless biographies. In court, some of these letters and Wilde's other writings were entered as evidence of what they allegedly communicated. Wilde desperately tried to make his accusers understand that the language of love letters and poetry has a function beyond that of merely conveying content. To be sure, Douglas's famous line of a "love that dare not speak its name" came up during the trial, and Victorian England's social and legal prohibitions of same-sex love are the lens through which all of Wilde's writings and behavior were scrutinized. But while defending himself against these prohibitions that made same-sex love so risky, Wilde also wanted the prosecutor and the public to understand that language can *create and transform* rather than merely *describe* reality. In the trial, Wilde's writings and speech were examined only for the content they were thought to convey. But Wilde's words, in spoken testimony, published works, and private letters, created new conditions for understanding them by effectively re-ordering reality. It is this newly ordered reality, shaped not by legal rulings and biographical facts alone but by the creative use of language, which we inhabit today.

Wilde did not succeed. In a bigoted legal expounding, the prosecutor interpreted Wilde's writings as covering up their true meaning, which he identified as homosexual desire. But Wilde's use of language as more than an instrument of communication should caution us from inadvertently following the prosecutor's lead. We should avoid his error and not decode Wilde's work as a veiled or metaphoric defense of same-sex love and a direct plea for social and political equality. Such an interpretation would once again miss Wilde's point: that the authentic expression of one's love is an irreducibly personal and creative act that can serve but must never be subordinated to a political program.

The present volume presents Oscar Wilde's letters to Lord Alfred Douglas alongside several relevant essays about their historical and literary significance to let today's readers enjoy the wit, joy, pain and passion that true love entails.

THE LETTERS OF OSCAR WILDE
TO LORD ALFRED DOUGLAS, 1892–1897

Love to Lincoln

Dearest Bosie

I am so
glad you are
better, and that
you like the
little cardross –
Oxford is
quite impossible
in winter – I

town – Tree rushing
up to see me
on all occasions –
also staging a
throbbing personality
weekly in painted
pageants –
Of the poem
I will write
tomorrow.

Oscar

go to Paris
next week – I
for 10 days or so away with
you and you really going
to the Sally
Isles ?

I should
awfully like to
get away with
you somewhere –
where it is hot
and coloured –
I am
terribly busy in

[circa November 1892]

Dearest Bosie,

I am so glad you are better, and that you like the little card-case—Oxford is quite impossible in winter. I go to Paris next week—for ten days or so. Are you really going to the Scilly Isles? I should awfully like to go away with you somewhere—where it is hot and coloured—

I am terribly busy in town. Tree running up to see me on all occasions—also strange and troubling personalities walking in painted pageants.

Of the poem I will write tomorrow.

Ever yours

OSCAR

Love to Encombe.

[circa January 1893]

[Babbacombe Cliff]

My Own Boy,

Your sonnet is quite lovely, and it is a marvel that those red rose-leaf lips of yours should have been made no less for music and song than for madness of kissing. Your slim gilt soul walks between passion and poetry. I know Hyacinthus, whom Apollo loved so madly, was you in Greek days.

Why are you alone in town, and when do you go to Salisbury? Do go there and cool your hands in the grey twilight of Gothic things, and come here whenever you like. It is a lovely place—it only lacks you; but go to Salisbury first.

Always, with undying love, yours

OSCAR

[circa February 1893]

Babbacombe Cliff

My dearest Bosie,

I have written to your man, and have received no reply from him—which is most annoying—as things are the wrong colour without gold to light them up—Are you working? I hope so—do get a good crammer—

I am rather unhappy as I can't write—I don't know why—things are all wrong. Have you been writing lovely sonnets? I never got the *Spirit-Lamp*—not even a cheque—!

My charge for the sonnet is £300. Who on earth *is* the Editor? He must be rented. I hear he is hiding at Salisbury.

With best love
Ever yours,

OSCAR

[March 1893]

Dearest of all Boys—

Your letter was delightful—red and yellow wine to me—but I am sad and out of sorts—Bosie—you must not make scenes with me—they kill me—they wreck the loveliness of life—I cannot see you, so Greek and gracious, distorted by passion; I cannot listen to your curved lips saying hideous things to me—don't do it—you break my heart—I'd sooner be rented all day, than have you bitter, unjust, and horrid—horrid—

I must see you soon—you are the divine thing I want—the thing of grace and genius—but I don't know how to do it—Shall I come to Salisbury—? There are many difficulties—my bill here is £49 for a week! I have also got a new sitting-room over the Thames—but you, why are you not here, my dear, my wonderful boy—? I fear I must leave; no money, no credit, and a heart of lead.

Ever your own,

OSCAR

[circa 12–15 April 1893]

Dearest Boy—

We have only just finished

Act 2!!

Dont wait

Order, of course, what you want. Lunch, 1.30 tomorrow: at Albemarle—I do not rehearse tomorrow at all.

Ever yours,

OSCAR

[circa May 1893]

My dear Boy,

No letter from you yet. But I hope to find a line when I go home—I lunched with Prince Troubetzkoi and Mrs Chanler this afternoon—He has done a lovely picture of her—and would do a beautiful one of you. I talked to him about you. He is going down to the Batterseas to finish his portrait of Cyril but will be back in the autumn. You really must be painted, and also have an ivory statue executed.

Willard, the actor, lunches with me on Thursday to talk business—I hope to lure him to give me some of "the gold the gryphon guards in rude Armenia."

Are you coming up on Wednesday: if so, do dine with me.

Ever yours

OSCAR

Saturday [9 September 1893]

My dear Bosie,

Thanks for your telegram which I got last night on my arrival from Jersey—where I had been for a night, on my way over, to see a performance of my play by Miss Lingard and the South Company—it was rather good, and I had a great reception from a crowded house—The General Arbuthnot was excellent, and very nice—I entertained the actors afterwards at supper—I am off to Goring now—to try and settle up things—I don't know what to do about the place—whether to stay there or not—and the servants are a worry—I went round to see Lane just now, but he is in Paris with Rothenstein—I hope you will get proofs soon—I suppose you are in Devon for your brother's marriage—give him my best wishes.

Ever yours,

OSCAR

[circa 20 December 1893]

10 & 11 St James's Place, London SW

My dearest Boy,

Thanks for your letter—I am overwhelmed by the wings of vulture creditors—and out of sorts—but I am happy in the knowledge that we are friends again—and that our love has passed through the shadow and the night of estrangement and sorrow and come out rose-crowned as of old—let us always be infinitely dear to each other, as indeed we have been always.

I hear Bobbie is in town—lame and bearded! Isn't it awful? I have not seen him yet. Lady Thompson has appeared—he is extremely anxious to devote his entire life to me—Tree has written a long apologetic letter—his reasons are so reasonable that I cannot understand them—a cheque is the only argument I recognize—Hare returns to town early next week. I am going to make an effort to induce him to see that my new play is a masterpiece—but I have grave doubts. This is all the news. How horrid news is! I think of you daily—and am always devotedly yours

Oscar

[circa 16 April 1894]

16 Tite Street

My dearest Boy,

Your telegram has just arrived—it was a joy to get it—but I miss you so much—the gay gilt and gracious lad has gone away—and hate every one else—they are tedious—also I am in the purple valleys of despair—and no gold coins are dropping down from heavens to gladden me—London is very dangerous—'Writters' come out at night and writ one—the roaring of creditors towards dawn is frightful—and solicitors are getting rabies and biting people—

How I envy you under Giotto's Tower, or sitting in the loggia looking at that green and gold god of Cellini's—You must write poems like apple blossoms—

The *Yellow Book* has appeared—it is dull and loathsome: a great failure—I am so glad.

Always, with much love, yours

OSCAR

[circa 20 April 1894]

16 Tite Street

My dearest Boy,

Life here is much the same—I find a chastened pleasure in being shaved in Air Street—you are always enquired after—and sonnet-like allusions made to your gilt silk hair. I saw an emissary from Mansfield, the actor, this morning. I think of writing *The Cardinal of Avignon* at once—If I had peace, I would do it. Mansfield would act it splendidly.

Max on Cosmetics in the *Yellow Book* is wonderful—: enough style for a large school—and all very precious and thought-out: quite delightfully wrong and fascinating.

I had a frantic telegram from Edward Shelley, of all people! asking me to see him. When he came he was of course in trouble for money—As he betrayed me grossly I, of course, gave him money and was kind to him. I find that forgiving one's enemies is a most curious morbid pleasure—perhaps I should check it.

With love

Every yours,

OSCAR

[circa July 1894]

My own dear Boy—

I hope the cigarettes arrived all right—I lunched with Gladys de Grey—Reggie and Aleck Yorke there. They want me to go to Paris with them on Thursday—they say one wears flannels and straw hats and dines in the Bois—but, of course, I have no money, as usual, and can't go—Besides I want to see you—It is really absurd—*I can't live without you*—You are so dear, so wonderful—I think of you all day long—and miss your grace, your boyish beauty, the bright sword-play of your wit, the delicate face of your genius, so surprising always in its sudden swallow-flights towards north or south, towards sun or moon—and, above all, you yourself. The only thing consoles me is what the Sybil of Mortimer Street (whom mortals term Mrs. Robinson—) said to me—if I could disbelieve her I would—but I can't—and I know that early in January you and I will go away together for a long voyage—and that your lovely life goes always hand in hand with mine—my dear wonderful boy, I hope you are brilliant and happy. I went to Bertie today I wrote at home—then went and sat with my mother—Death and Love seem to walk on either hand as I go through life—They are the only things I think of—their winds shadow me.

London is a desert without your dainty feet, and all the but-tonholes have turned to weeds—nettles and hemlock are 'the only

13

wear'—Write me a line, and take all my love—now and for ever.

Always, and with devotion,—but I have no words for how I love you—

Oscar

[July–August 1894]

16 Tite Street

Dearest Boy,

I hope to send you the cigarettes—if Simmonds will let me have them—

He has applied for his bill—I am overdrawn £41 at the Bank— it really is intolerable the want of money—I have not a penny—I can't stand it any longer—but don't know what to do—I go down to Worthing tomorrow—I hope to do work there. The house, I hear, is very small—and I have no writing room—However, anything is better than London—

Your father is on the rampage again—been to Café Royal to enquire for us—with threats etc. I think now it would have been better for me to have had him bound over to keep the peace—but what a scandal! Still, it is intolerable to be dogged by a maniac—

When you come to Worthing of course all things will be done for your honour and joy—but I fear you may find the meals etc. tedious. But you will come—won't you? at any rate for a short time—till you are bored.

Ernesto has written to me begging for money—a very nice letter—but I really have nothing, just now.

What purple valleys of despair one goes through! Fortunately there is one person in the world to love.

Ever yours,

OSCAR

[August 1894]

[The Haven, 5 Esplanade, Worthing]

Dearest Bosie,

I have just come in from luncheon—A horrid ugly Swiss governess has, I find, been looking after Cyril and Vivian for a year—she is quite impossible.

Also children at meals are tedious—

Also, you, the gilt and graceful boy, would be bored—

Don't come here—I will come to you.

Ever yours,

OSCAR

My own dearest Boy,

How sweet of you to send me that charming poem—I can't tell you how it touches me—and it is full of that light lyrical grace that you always have—a quality that seems so easy, to those who don't understand how difficult it is to make the white feet of poetry dance lightly among flowers without crushing them—and to those "who know" is so rare and so distinguished. I have been doing nothing here but bathing and play writing—My play is really very funny—I am quite delighted with it—But it is not shaped yet. It lies in Sibylline leaves around the room—and Arthur has twice made a chaos of it by 'tidying up'—The result, however, was rather dramatic—I am inclined to think that Chaos is a stronger evidence for an Intelligent Creator than Kosmos is: the view might be expanded.

Percy left the day after you did. He spoke much of you— Alphonso is still in favor—He is my only companion—along with Steven—Alphonso always alludes to you as 'The Lord'—which however gives you I think a Biblical Hebraic dignity that gracious Greek boys should *not* have—He also says from time to time, 'Percy was the Lord's favourite' which makes me think of Percy as the infant Samuel—an inaccurate reminiscence as Percy was Hellenic.

Yesterday (Sunday) Alphonso, Stephen, and I sailed to Littlehampton in the morning—bathing on the way—We took five hours in an awful gale to come back! did not reach the pier till eleven o'clock at night—pitch dark all the way—and a fearful sea—I was drenched, but was Viking-like and daring. It was, however, quite a dangerous adventure—All the fishermen were waiting for us—I flew to the hotel for hot brandy and water—on landing with my companions—and found a letter for you from dear Henry, which I send you—They had forgotten to forward it—as it was past *ten* o'clock on a Saturday night the proprietor could not *sell* us any brandy or spirits of any kind! So he had to *give* it to us. The result was not displeasing, but what laws! An hotel proprietor is not allowed to sell 'necessary harmless' alcohol to three shipwrecked mariners—wet to the skin—because it is Sunday! Both Alphonso and Stephen are now anarchists—I need hardly say.

Your new Sibyl is really wonderful—It is most extraordinary—I must meet her—

Dear, dear boy—you are more to me than any one of them has any idea—You are the atmosphere of beauty through which I see life—you are the incarnation of all lovely things—When we are out of tune—all colour goes from things for me—but we are never really out of tune—I think of you day and night.

Write to me soon—you honey-haired boy!—I am always devotedly yours

OSCAR

[8 September 1894]

5 Esplanade, Worthing

My own dear Boy,

Your sweet letter arrived this morning—and this moment I have received your delightful telegram—delightful, because I love you to think of me—What do you think of three days at Dieppe? I have a sort of longing for France—and with you—if you can manage to come—; (I could only arrange three days—as I am so busy—)

I went yesterday up to town for the afternoon—lunched with George Alexander at the Garrick—got a little money from him—and returned by the 4.30 for dinner—so I can pay my rent, and Cyril's—(little wretch and darling,) school-fees—I dare not lodge the money in the Bank, as I have overdrawn £40—but I think of hiding gold in the garden—

Could you meet me at Newhaven on the 15th?—Dieppe is very amusing and bright. Or would you come down here first—say on Thursday: and we cd. go on?

I saw Gatby, by chance, as I was driving through Pall Mall—he stopped my cab—we had a long chat: about *you*, of course. He is one of your many admirers—Last night (see other letter)—you, and I, and the mayor figured as patrons for the entertainment given by the vagabond singers of the sands—They told me that our names, which have been placarded, all over the town, excited great enthusiasm—and certainly the Hall was crammed—I was greeted with loud applause, as I entered with Cyril: Cyril was considered to be you—

Dear boy—this is a scrawl is it not? I find farcical comedies admirable for style, but fatal to handwriting—

Do write to me—and do come to France—Is Basil *here*? If so, of course, come here—with fondest love, ever devotedly yours,

OSCAR

[5 or 6 November 1894]

16 Tite Street

My dearest Bosie,

I suppose you won't come up now, it is so late. Perhaps I shall hear tomorrow. I can't bear your sadness and unhappiness: because I cannot cure it. But you know what a joy it will be to see you again. I have been staying at Cannizaro from Saturday to Monday: Noel Holland, one of Knutford's sons, was there: he is partner with Edward Arnold the publisher: I told him of our idea of writing a book *How to Live Above one's Income—for the Use of the Sons of the Rich:* he was charmed: he seems very mad, but is quite brilliant: one of Ames's with his fiancée was there also: there were many affectionate enquiries after you—Tiny was sweet as usual: Mrs Schuster had a black eye! a fall from her donkey-chaise: She was swathed in lace, jewels, and flowers: quite extraordinary to look at.

I heard all the details of the divorce of the Scarlet Marquis the other day: quite astonishing: Arthur Pollen told me all about it: he came to tea one afternoon.

Surely your mother intends to give you a good allowance now—when she is a little better I feel certain she will: it should be about £400 or £500 a year. It is absurd you should not have an allowance suitable to your position. I think you should speak to your mother about it, before you come up.

On Thursday night I am going to the first night of Tree's new play: so if you are in town I suppose you will dine with Robbie: or some other friend.

I am sending you a copy of *Hafiz* the divinest of poets—I hope the honey of his verse may charm you.

London is dripping with rain: a loathsome day.

Ever, with much love, yours,

OSCAR

[circa 9 November 1894]

Albemarle Club

My dearest Boy,

I have been very lonely without you: and worried by money matters. Today is golden enough, but rain has dripped monotonously on all other days.

I went to Haddon Chamber's play: it was not bad, but oh! so badly written! The bows and salutations of the lower orders who thronged the stalls were so cold that I felt it my duty to sit in the Royal Box with Ribblesdales, the Harry Whites, and the Home Secretary: This exasperated the wretches. How strange to live in a land where the worship of beauty, and the passion of love are considered infamous—I hate England: it is only bearable to me because you are here.

Last night I supped at Willis': There were respectful enquiries after 'Lord Douglas'—Always yours

Oscar

[circa 17 February 1895]

Thos Cook & Son, 33 Piccadilly

Dearest Boy,

Yes! The Scarlet Marquis made a plot to address the audience on the first night of my play!!

Algy Burke revealed it—and he was not allowed to enter.

He left a grotesque bouquet of vegetables for me! This of course makes his conduct idiotic—robs it of dignity.

He arrived with a prize-fighter!! I had all Scotland Yard— twenty police—to guard the theatre. He prowled about for three hours—then left chattering like a monstrous ape—Percy is on our side.

I feel now that, without your name being mentioned, all will go well.

I had not wished you to know—Percy wired without telling me—I am greatly touched by [your] rushing over Europe—For my own part I had determined you shd. know nothing.

I will wire to Calais and Dover—and you will of course stay with me till Saturday. I then return to Tite St, I think.

Ever, with love, all love in the world, devotedly yours

OSCAR

[5 April 1895]

[Cadogan Hotel]

My dear Bosie,

I will be at Bow Street Police Station tonight—no bail possible I am told. Will you ask Percy, and George Alexander, and Waller, at the Haymarket, to attend to give bail.

Would you also wire Humphreys to appear at Bow Street for me, Wire to 41 Norfolk Square, W.

Also, come to see me. Ever yours

OSCAR

Monday Evening [29 April 1895]

HM Prison, Holloway

My dearest boy,

   This is to assure you of my immortal, my eternal love for you. Tomorrow all will be over. If prison and dishonour be my destiny, think that my love for you and this idea, this still more divine belief, that you love me in return will sustain me in my unhappiness and will make me capable, I hope, of bearing my grief most patiently. Since the hope, nay rather the certainty, of meeting you again in some world is the goal and the encouragement of my present life, ah! I must continue to live in this world because of that.

   Dear [   ] came to see me today. I gave him several messages for you. He told me one thing that reassured me: that my mother should never want for anything. I have always provided for her subsistence, and the thought that she might have to suffer privations was making me unhappy. As for you (graceful boy with a Christlike heart), as for you, I beg you, as soon as you have done all that you can, leave for Italy and regain your calm, and write those lovely poems which you do with such a strange grace. Do not expose yourself to England for any reason whatsoever. If one day, at Corfu or in some enchanted isle, there were a little house where we could live together, oh! life would be sweeter than it has ever been. Your love has broad wings and is strong, your love comes to me through my prison bars and comforts me, your love is the light of all my hours. Those who know not what love is will write, I know, if fate is against us, that I have had a bad influence upon your life. If they do that, you shall write, you shall say in your turn, that it is not so. Our love was always beautiful and noble, and if I have been the butt of a terrible tragedy, it is because the nature of that love has not been understood. In your letter this morning you say something which gives me courage. I must remember it. You write that it is my duty to you and to myself to live in spite of everything. I think that is true. I shall try and I shall do it. I want you to keep Mr Humphreys informed of your movements so that when he comes he can tell me what you are doing. I believe solicitors are allowed to see the prisoners fairly often. Thus I could communicate with you.

I am so happy that you have gone away! I know what that must have cost you. It would have been agony for me to think that you were in England when your name was mentioned in court. I hope you have copies of all my books. All mine have been sold. I stretch out my hands towards you. Oh! may I live to touch your hair and your hands. I think that your love will watch over my life. If I should die, I want you to live a gentle peaceful existence somewhere, with flowers, pictures, books, and lots of work. Try to let me hear from you soon. I am writing you this letter in the midst of great suffering; this long day in court has exhausted me. Dearest boy, sweetest of all young men, most loved and most loveable. Oh! wait for me! wait for me! I am now, as ever since the day we met, yours devoutly and with an immortal love

OSCAR

[May 1895]

As for you, you have given me the beauty of life in the past, and in the future if there is any future. That is why I shall be eternally grateful to you for having always inspired me with adoration and love. Those days of pleasure were our dawn. Now, in anguish and pain, in grief and humiliation, I feel that my love for you, your love for me, are the two signs of my life, the divine sentiments which make all bitterness bearable. Never has anyone in my life been dearer than you, never has any love been greater, more sacred, more beautiful.

Dear boy, among pleasures or in prison, you and the thought of you were everything to me. Oh! keep me always in your heart; you are never absent from mine. I think of you much more than of myself, and if, sometimes, the thought of horrible and infamous suffering comes to torture me, the simple thought of you is enough to strengthen me and heal my wounds. Let destiny, Nemesis, or the unjust gods alone receive the blame for everything that has happened.

Every great love has its tragedy, and now ours has too, but to have known and loved you with such profound devotion, to have had you for a part of my life, the only part I now consider beautiful, is enough for me. My passion is at a loss for words, but you can understand me, you alone. Our souls were made for one another, and by knowing yours through love, mine has transcended many evils, understood perfection, and entered into the divine essence of things.

Pain, if it comes, cannot last for ever; surely one day you and I will meet again, and though my face be a mask of grief and my body worn out by solitude, you and you alone will recognize the soul which is more beautiful for having met yours, the soul of the artist who found this ideal in you, of the lover of beauty to whom you appeared as a being flawless and perfect. Now I think of you as a golden-haired boy with Christ's own heart in you. I know now how much greater love is than everything else. You have taught me the divine secret of the world.

[20 May 1895]

[circa 2 Courtfield Gardens, Kensington]

My child,

Today it was asked to have the verdicts rendered separately.
Taylor is probably being judged at this moment, so that I have been
able to come back here. My sweet rose, my delicate flower, my lily
of lilies, it is perhaps in prison that I am going to test the power
of love. I am going to see if I cannot make the bitter waters sweet
by the intensity of the love I bear you. I have had moments when
I thought it would be wiser to separate. Ah! moments of weakness
and madness! Now I see that that would have mutilated my life,
ruined my art, broken the musical chords which make a perfect
soul. Even covered with mud I shall praise you, from the deepest
abysses I shall cry to you. In my solitude you will be with me. I am
determined not to revolt but to accept every outrage through devotion to love, to let my body be dishonoured so long as my soul may
always keep the image of you. From your silken hair to your delicate
feet you are perfection to me. Pleasure hides love from us but pain
reveals it in its essence. O dearest of created things, if someone
wounded by silence and solitude comes to you, dishonoured, a
laughing-stock to men, oh! you can close his wounds by touching
them and restore his soul which unhappiness had for a moment
smothered. Nothing will be difficult for you then, and remember,
it is that hope which makes me live, and that hope alone. What

31

wisdom is to the philosopher, what God is to his saint, you are to me. To keep you in my soul, such is the goal of this pain which men call life. O my love, you whom I cherish above all things, white narcissus in an unmown field, think of the burden which falls to you, a burden which love alone can make light. But be not saddened by that, rather be happy to have filled with an immortal love the soul of a man who now weeps in hell, and yet carries heaven in his heart. I love you, I love you, my heart is a rose which your love has brought to bloom, my life is a desert fanned by the delicious breeze of your breath, and whose cool springs are your eyes; the imprint of your little feet makes valleys of shade for me, the odour of your hair is like myrrh, and wherever you go you exhale the perfumes of the cassia tree.

Love me always, love me always. You have been the supreme, the perfect love of my life; there can be no other.

I decided that it was nobler and more beautiful to stay. We could not have been together. I did not want to be called a coward or a deserter. A false name, a disguise, a hunted life, all that is not for me, to whom you have been revealed on that high hill where beautiful things are transfigured.

O sweetest of all boys, most loved of all loves, my soul clings to your soul, my life is your life, and in all the worlds of pain and pleasure you are my ideal of admiration and joy.

OSCAR

[2 June 1897]

Hôtel de la Plage, Berneval-sur-Mer

My dear Boy,

If you *will* send me back beautiful letters, with bitter ones of your own, of course you will never remember my address—It is as above.

Of Lugné-Poe, of course, I know nothing except that he is singularly handsome, and seems to me to have the personality of a good actor, for personality does not require intellect to help it: it is a dynamic force of its own, and is often as superbly unintelligent as the great forces of nature, like the lightning that shook at sudden moments last night over the sea that slept before my window.

The production of *Salomé* was the thing that turned the scale in my favour, as far as my treatment in prison by the Government was concerned, and I am deeply grateful to all concerned in it. Upon the other hand I could not give my next play for nothing, as I simply do not know how I shall live after the summer is over unless I at once make money—I am in a terrible and dangerous position—for money that I had been assured was set aside for me, was not forthcoming when I wanted it. It was a horrible disappointment: for I have of course begun to live as a man of letters should live—that is with a private sitting room and books and the like. I can see no other way of living, if I am to write, though I can see many others, if I am not.

If then Lugné-Poe can give me no money, of course I shall not consider myself bound to him. But the play in question—being religious in surroundings and treatment of subject—is not a play for a *run*, at all. Three performances are the most I think I could expect. All I want is to have my artistic reappearance, and own rehabilitation through art, in *Paris*, not in London. It is a homage and a debt I owe to that great city of art.

If anyone else with money would take the play, and let Lugné-Poe play the part, I would be more than content. In any case I am not bound, and, what is of more import, the play is not written! I am still trying to finish my necessary correspondence, and to express suitably my deep gratitude to all who have been kind to me.

As regards *Le Journal*, I have the chance to write for it, and will try and get it regularly—I do not like to *abonner* myself at the office as I am anxious that my address should not be known—I think I had better do it at Dieppe, from where I get the *Echo de Paris?*

I hear the *Jour* has had a sort of interview—a false one—with you. This is very distressing: as much, I don't doubt, to you as me. I hope however that it is not the cause of the duel you hint at— Once you get to fight duels in France, you have to be always doing it, and it is a nuisance. I do hope that you will always shelter yourself under the accepted right of any English gentleman to decline a duel—unless of course some personal fracas or public insult takes place.

Of course you will never dream of fighting a duel for *me*: that would be awful, and create the worst and most odious impression.

Always write to me about your art and the art of others. It is better to meet on the double peak of Parnassus than elsewhere—I have read your poems with great pleasure and interest: but on the whole your best work is to me still the work you did two years and a half ago—the ballads, the bits of the play: of course your own personality has had for many reasons to express itself *directly* since then, but I hope you will go on to forms more remote from any actual events and passions—

One can really, as I say in *Intentions,* be far more subjective in an *objective* form than in any other way. If I were asked of myself as a dramatist, I would say that my unique position was that I had taken the Drama, the most objective form known to art, and made it as personal a mode of expression as the Lyric or the Sonnet, while enriching the characterization of the stage, and enlarging—at any rate in the case of *Salomé*—its artistic horizon. You have real sympathy with the Ballad. Pray again return to it. The Ballad is the true origin of the romantic Drama, and the true predecessors of Shakespeare are not the tragic writers of the Greek or Latin Stage, from Aeschylus to Seneca, but the ballad-writers of the Border—In such a ballad as *Gilderoy* one has the prefiguring note of the romance of *Romeo and Juliet,* different though the plots are. The recurring phrases of *Salomé,* that bind it together like a piece of music with recurring motifs, are, and were to me, the artistic equivalent of the refrains of old ballads. All this is to beg you to write ballads.

I do not know whether I have to thank you or More for the books from Paris—probably both. As I have divided the books, so you must divide the thanks—

I am greatly fascinated by the *Napoléon* of La Jeunesse. He must be most interesting. André Gide's book fails to fascinate me. The egoistic note is, of course, and has always been to me, the primal and ultimate note of modern art, but *to be an Egoist one must have an Ego.* It is not everyone who says 'I, I' who can enter into the Kingdom of Art. But I love André personally very deeply, and often thought of him in prison, as I often did of dear Reggie

Cholmondeley, with his large Faun's eyes and honey-sweet smile. Given him my fondest love.

Ever yours

OSCAR

Kindly forward enclosed card to Reggie, with my address. Tell him to keep *both* a secret.

Thursday [3 June 1897] 2:30

[Hôtel de la Plage, Berneval-sur-Mer]

My dear Boy,

I have just received three copies of *Le Jour,* that I ordered from
Dieppe; not knowing what day the supposed interview with you
had taken place, I had ordered the numbers for Friday, Saturday,
and Sunday.

The interview is quite harmless, and I am really sorry you took
any notice of it. I *do* hope it is not with the low-class journalist that
you are to fight; if that absurd experience is in store for you—If you
ever fight in France let it be with someone who *exists.* To fight with
the dead is either vulgar farce, or a revolting tragedy.

Let me know by telegram if anything has happened. The telegraph office is at Dieppe, but they send out on swift bicycles men
in fantastic dresses of the middle-*class* age—who blow horns all the
time so that the moon shall hear them.

The costume of the *moyen-age* is lovely, but the dress of the mid-
dle-*class* age is dreadful.

Let me beg one thing of you. Please *always* let me see *anything*
that appears about myself in the Paris papers—good or bad, but
especially the bad. It is a matter of vital import to me to know the
attitude of the community. All mystery enrages me, and when dear

More wrote to say that a false interview with you of no importance had been published, I hired a *voiture* at once and galloped to Dieppe to try and find it—and ordered, as I have told you, three separate numbers. It wrecks my nerves to think of things appearing on me that are kept from me. If More had enclosed it in his letter, I would have been happy and satisfied. As it was, I was really unnerved. The smallest word about me tells.

If *Le Journal* would publish my letter to the *Daily Chronicle* it would be a great thing for me. I hope you have seen it.

Ernest Dowson, Conder, and Dal Young—what a name—are coming out to dine and sleep—at least I know they dine, but I believe they don't sleep.

Ever yours,

OSCAR

Friday [4 June 1897] 2.30

[Hôtel de la Plage, Berneval-sur-Mer]

My dear Boy,

I have just got your letter, but Ernest Dowson, Dal Young, and Conder are here, so I cannot read it—except the last three lines—I love the last words of any thing: the end in art is the beginning. Don't think I don't love you. Of course I love [you] more than anyone else. But our lives are irreparably severed, as far as meeting goes. What is left to us is the knowledge that we love each other—and every day I think of you, and I know you are a poet, and that makes you doubly dear and wonderful—My friends here have been most sweet to me, and I like them all very much—Young is the best of fellows, and Ernest has a most interesting nature. He is to send me some of his work.

We all stayed up till 3 o'clock—very bad for me—but it was a delightful experience—

Today is a day of sea-fog, and rain—my first. Tomorrow I go with fishers to fish—but I will write to you tonight.

Ever, dear boy, with fondest love.

Oscar

Sunday night, 6 June [1897]

[Hôtel de la Plage, Berneval-sur-Mer]

My dearest Boy,

I must give up this *absurd* habit of writing to you every day. It comes of course from the strange new joy of talking to you daily. But next week I must make a resolution to write to you only every seven days, and then on the question of the relations of the sonnet to modern life, and the importance of your writing romantic ballads, and the strange beauty of that lovely line of Rossetti's, suppressed till lately by his brother, where he says that, 'the sea ends in a sad blueness beyond rhyme.' Don't you think it lovely? 'In a sad *blueness* beyond thyme.' *Voilà 'l'influence du bleu dans les arts,'* with a vengeance!

I am so glad you went to bed at 7 o'clock. Modern life is terrible to vibrating delicate frames like yours—a rose-leaf in a storm of hard hail is not so fragile. With us who are modern it is the *scabbard* that wears out the sword.

Will you do this for me—get *Le Courier de la Presse* to procure a copy of *Le Soir,* the *Brussels* paper, somewhere between the 26th and the 31st of May last—which has an article on my letter to the *Chronicle,* a translation of it, I believe, and notice—It is of vital importance for me to have it as soon as possible. My *Chronicle* letter is to be published as a pamphlet with a postscript—and I need the *Soir*. I don't want to write myself for it, for obvious reasons. Dear boy, I hope you are still sweetly asleep—you are so absurdly sweet when you are asleep. I have been to Mass at ten o'clock and to Vespers at three o'clock I was a little bored by a sermon in the morning, but Benediction was delightful. I am seated in the Choir! I suppose sinners should have the high places near Christ's altar? I know at any rate that Christ would not turn me out.

Remember, after a few days, only *one letter a week*—I *must* school myself to it.

En attendant, Yours with all love

OSCAR

Poète-forçat

Tuesday, 15 June [1897]

Berneval-sur-Mer

My own dear Boy,

Who posts your letters? Does anyone? Or do you ever really know the day of the month? I rarely do myself, and Ernest Dowson, who is here, never.

The reason of these tedious questions is that last night on coming from Argues-la-Bataille where I had been breakfasting with Ernest, I found a letter from you *dated June 11*. (That is last *Friday)* but *posted* June 13 (last Sunday.) I have kept the envelope for you.

You ask me in it to let you come on Saturday: but dear honey-sweet boy I have already asked you to come then: so we both have the same desire, as usual.

Your name is to be Jonquil du Vallon.

Will you write *at once* to Edward Strangman, Hôtel Terminus, Gare St Lazare, to say you would like to see him and have news of me. He is a very gentle, rather shy chap: Irish by race, Oxford by culture: a friend of Will Rothenstein and Robbie, and a good friend of mine: he has just sent me lovely books I needed: pray let him know that I was so touched and pleased by his visit.

I suppose I shall hear at length from you today: the *facteur* comes at twelve o'clock and leaves at once, so all I can ever write in immediate response is a green-gray postcard. Only wine will induce the Facteur to wait. Nothing else has any influence with him.

Always devotedly yours

Oscar

Wednesday, 16 June [1897]

Berneval-sur-Mer

My dear Boy,

I am upset with the idea that you don't get my letters, or that the post goes wrong, or something. I daresay it is all absurd, but your last three letters dated the 10th, 11th, and 12th (whereas we are now at the 16th) contain no references to things I asked you, especially as regards our meeting.

I have asked you to come here on Sunday: I have a bathing costume for you, but you had better get one in Paris. Also bring me a lot of books, and cigarettes. I cannot get good cigarettes here or at Dieppe.

The weather is very hot, so you will want a straw hat and flannels. I hope you will get quietly out of Paris. On arriving at Dieppe, take a good voiture and tell him to drive to the Hôtel *Bonnet*, Berneval-sur-Mer, and go by the road by *Puys*, not the *grande route* which is a straight line of white dust.

If you want a café at Dieppe on arriving, go to the Café Suisse.

It takes an hour and a half to get here, so arrive if you can at Dieppe about three o'clock and be here at five o'clock.

I hope to be in my chalet by Saturday: so you will stay with me there. I have a little walled-in place in the garden of the hotel where I have *déjeuner* and *diner*—a *bosquet* of trees.

On Sunday I go to Mass, in a dark blue suit.

You must not have your letters sent on under your own name. It might do me serious harm. I will suggest—for the third time—Jonquil du Vallon, but any name you like will do.

Pray do not fail to write at once on receipt of this, and be careful of the date. Your *last* letter is dated the 12th; which was last *Saturday*.

It is lovely here today, and I am going to bathe at 10.30. Yesterday I drove Ernest Dowson back to Arques. I like him immensely.

Thanks for the *Soir:* you ask me other questions in your letter that I have answered in letters of my own to you: but I don't know if they reach you. I will wait for today's post, and write again tomorrow.

Bring also some perfume and nice things from the sellers of the dust of roses.

Also bring yourself.

Ever yours

OSCAR

Thursday, 17 June [1897] 2 o'clock p.m.

Café Suisse, Dieppe

My dearest Boy,

I have been obliged to ask my friends to leave me, as I am so upset and distressed in nerve by my solicitor's letter, and the apprehension of serious danger, that simply I must be alone. I find that any worry utterly destroys my health, and makes me horrid and irritable and unkind, though I hate to be so.

Of course at present it is impossible for us to meet. I have to find out what grounds my solicitor has for his sudden action, and of course if your father—or rather Q as I only know him and think of him—if Q came over and made a scene and scandal it would utterly destroy my possible future and alienate all my friends from me. I owe to my friends everything, including the clothes I wear, and I would be wretched if I did anything that would separate them from me.

So simply we must write to each other: about the things we love, about poetry and the coloured arts of our age, and that passage of ideas into images that is the intellectual history of art. I think of you always, and love you always, but chasms of moonless nights divide us. We cannot cross it without hideous and nameless peril.

Later on, when the alarm in England is over, when secrecy is possible, and silence forms part of the world's attitude, we may meet, but at present you see it is impossible. I would be harassed, agitated, nervous. It would be no joy for me to let you see me as I am now.

You must go to some place where you can play golf and get back your lily and rose. Don't, like a good boy, telegraph to me unless on a matter of vital import: the telegraph office is seven miles off, and I have to pay the *facteur*, and also reply, and yesterday with three separate *facteurs*, and three separate replies, I was *sans le sou*, and also mentally upset in nerve. Say please to Percy that I will accept a bicycle with many thanks for his kindness: I want to get it here, where there is a great champion who teaches everyone, and has English machines: it will cost £15. If Percy will send me £15 to enclosed name and address in a cheque, it will make me very happy. Send him my card.

Ever yours (rather maimed and mutilated)

OSCAR

Wednesday, June 23 [1897]

My darling Boy,

Thanks for your letter received this morning: my *fête* was a huge success: fifteen *gamins* were entertained on strawberries and cream, apricots, chocolates, cakes and *sirop de grenadine*—I had a huge iced cake with *Jubilé de la Reine Victoria* in pink sugar just rosetted with green, and a great wreath of red roses round it all. Every child was asked beforehand to choose his present: they all chose instruments of music!!!

6 accordions
5 trompettes
4 clairons—

They sang the Marseillaise and other songs, and danced a *ronde*, and also played 'God save the Queen': they said it was 'God save the Queen,' and I did not like to differ from them. They also all had flags which I gave them. They were most gay, and sweet. I gave the health of *La Reine d'Angleterre,* and they cried *'Vive la Reine d'Angleterre!!!!'* Then I gave *'La France'—mère de tous les artistes'*—and finally I gave *Le Président de la République* I thought I had better do so—They cried out with one accord *'Vivent le Président de la République et Monsieur Melmoth'!!!* So I found my name coupled with that of the President—it was an amusing experience as I am hardly more than a month out of goal.

They stayed from 4.30 to seven o'clock and played games: on leaving I gave them each a basket with a jubilee cake frosted pink and inscribed, and bonbons—

They seem to have made a great demonstration in Berneval-le-Grand, and to have gone to the House of the Mayor and cried *'Vive Monsieur Le Maire! Vive la Reine d'Angleterre! Vive Monsieur Melmoth!'*—I tremble at my position—

Today I have come in with Ernest Dowson to dine with the painter Thaulow—a giant with the temperament of Corot—I sleep here and go back tomorrow.

I will write tomorrow on things.

Ever, dearest boy, your

OSCAR

Wednesday 7 [July 1897]

Café Suisse, Dieppe

My darling Boy,

I received your letters all right and have half written my answer—

I write now on nicer things: just to know how you are, and why you stay at a place that bores you—I hear from Ernest Dowson that Montigny-sur-Loire is lovely, and full of dear brilliant artists and sweet people. Stuart Merrill lives at Marlotte—only 3 miles off—and of course is charming and sympathetic. I hate to know you are lonely, or in danger of *ennui* that enemy of modern life.

I am waiting here for a new servant—sent to me from Avesnes—I have not yet seen him, but I hope he will be nice.

He is to come here to find me. Brutes, bald and bearded, have arrived—and Ernest Dowson says he is sure my servant is among them. It is so awful, that I am going to deny I am M. Sebastian Melmoth—

Tell me about your days. Is Gaston in waiting? Are you writing anything? Whom have you met?

Tomorrow I am going to write my poem—I will send it to you.

With my love, dearest boy,
Ever your

Oscar

Do you know Hugues Rebell? He has just sent me his book, *Nichina.* Also Tristan Klingson? who sends poems. His name is so lovely I fear I shall be disappointed with his work. In fact I am.

Tuesday, 7.30 [circa 31 August 1897]

Café Suisse, Dieppe

My own darling Boy,

I got your telegram half an hour ago—and just send you a line to say that I feel that my only hope of again doing beautiful work in art is being with you—It was not so in old days—but now it is different, and you can really recreate in me that energy and sense of joyous power on which Art depends—Everyone is furious with me for going back to you—but they don't understand us—I feel that it is only with you that I can do anything at all—Do remake my ruined life for me—and then our friendship and love will have a different meaning to the world—

I wish that when we met at Rouen we had not parted at all—There are such wide abysses now of space and land between us—But we love each other—

Good night—dear—
Ever yours

OSCAR

[circa 12 September 1897]

[Dieppe]

My dearest boy,

I hope to go to Naples in three days, but I must try and get some more money. I see it costs £10 to go to Naples. This is awful. Of course, wait until your cure is finished. I hope you will have no more rheumatic horrors. I know how dreadful they are.

As regards Venice, of course do just as you will, but the sooner you come to Naples the happier I shall be. At present I am wretched and in low spirits. Come as soon as you can. The accumulated hotel bills were awful, and the proprietress, of course, turned out to be a Shylock.

Ever yours, with love

OSCAR

Wednesday
May 15th
1908

My darling Bou

Have just arrived here & it seems too dreadful to be here without you, but I hope you will join me here next week. Dieppe was too awful for anything, it is the most depressing place in the world, even Petit chevaux was not to be had, as the Casino was closed. They are very nice here, & I can stay as long as I like, without paying my bill which is a good thing & I am quite penniless. The proprietor is very nice & most sympathetic, he asked after you at once & expressed his regret & indignation at the treatment you had

received. I shall have to send this & a card to the gare du nord to catch the post as I want you to get it first post tomorrow. I am going to see if I can find Robert Sherard tomorrow. If he is in Paris, Charlie is in the rue & sends you his best love. I had a long letter of Robbie this morning about you. Do keep up your spirits my dearest darling & continue to think of you day & night, & I send you all my love. I am always your own loving & devoted boy

Bosie

Letter from Alfred Douglas to Oscar Wilde

[15 May 1895]

My darling Oscar,

Have just arrived here. It seems too dreadful to be here without you, but I hope you will join me here next week. Dieppe was too awful for anything, it is the most depressing place in the world, even Petits Chevaux was not [to] be had, as the Casino was closed. They are very nice here, and I can stay as long as I like without paying my bill which is a good thing as I am quite penniless. The proprietor is very nice and *most* sympathetic, he asked after you at once & expressed his great indignation at the treatment you had received. I shall have to send this by a cab to the Gare du Nord to catch the post as I want you to get it first post tomorrow.

I am going to see if I can find Robert Sherard tomorrow if he is in Paris.

Charlie is with me and sends you his best love.

I had a long letter from More this morning about you. Do keep up your spirits my dearest darling, I continue to think of you day & night, and I send you all my love.

I am always your own loving & devoted boy

BOSIE

NOTES ON THE LETTERS

These notes appear in Clark's edition of *Letters from Oscar Wilde to Lord Alfred Douglas, 1892–1897*. Date references have been corrected in some cases and are now available in Merlin Holland and Rupert Hart-Davis, eds., *The Complete Letters of Oscar Wilde* (New York: Henry Holt, 2000), which the present volume follows.

PAGE 5: [CIRCA FEBRUARY 1893]
Written while Lord Alfred Douglas was an undergraduate at Oxford and the editor of the student publication, *The Spirit Lamp*. The sonnet of which Oscar Wilde writes is "The New Remorse," which he gave Douglas for publication and which appeared in that magazine in the issue of December 6, 1892; the prose poem, "The House of Judgment," appeared in the issue of February 17, 1893, pp. 51–53.

An earlier version of "The New Remorse," under the title of "Un Amant des Nos Jours," had been published in the *Court and Society Review* for December 13, 1887.

A third contribution to "The Spirit Lamp" was made by Wilde while Douglas was still editor, namely the prose poem, "The Disciple," appearing in that issue of June, 1893, pp. 49–50.

Babbacombe, from which place this letter is written, is a small bathing and boating resort just outside of Torquay on the south coast of England between Exeter and Plymouth.

The term "rented" was a slang phrase in use at the time, implying blackmail. That this use of the word was not unfamiliar to Wilde is shown by its appearing in a letter to Douglas which was read and made part of the record in the libel action brought by Wilde against the Marquis of Queensberry, the father of Lord Alfred Douglas. (See *Oscar Wilde*, by Frank Harris [1916], vol. I, p. 209.)

PAGE 7: [CIRCA 12–15 APRIL 1893]
The rehearsal mentioned in the letter refers without doubt to one of Wilde's comedies, *A Woman of No Importance*, produced at the Haymarket Theater, London, April 19, 1893. It is improbable that it refers to a rehearsal for one of the two plays which Wilde produced early in 1895, for from one of the later letters herein published, it appears that Douglas was abroad in February, 1985, and the words in this letter, "Order, of course, what you want," do not comport with the protestations of impecuniosity which run through the letters of the later time.

PAGE 8: [CIRCA MAY 1893]
There are numerous mentions of Cyril, Wilde's eldest son, in the letters of the summer of 1894 which follow, but no reference is there to a portrait of the boy by Troubetzkoi. Indeed from Wilde's almost bankrupt state in 1894, it is doubtful if he would have commissioned the painting during that summer or in the preceding spring.

The reference to "Willard, the actor" is undoubtedly to E. S. Willard. From the type of characters played by Willard it is probable that Wilde was trying to interest him in his projected play around the Cardinal of Avignon which he later offered to Richard Mansfield.

PAGE 9: [9 SEPTEMBER 1893]
This letter can be definitely placed as of September, 1893, by its last

sentence: "I suppose you are in Devon for your brother's marriage," etc., which unquestionably refers to the marriage of Lord Alfred Douglas's older brother, Percy Sholto Douglas to Hannah Maria Walters on September 11, 1893.

The performance referred to is one by a provincial company, of Wilde's comedy, *A Woman of No Importance*.

During the summer of 1893, Wilde had maintained an establishment at Goring, a resort on the Thames between London and Oxford.

PAGE 10: [CIRCA 20 DECEMBER 1893]

The new play mentioned, probably the comedy *An Ideal Husband*, written during the summer, is finished and Wilde is back in London attempting to make arrangements for its production.

Arrangements for the production of *The Importance of Being Earnest* had already been made with Alexander, so the "new play" mentioned could not be this, but must be the former to which the allusion is made. This is supported by the fact that either Hare or Tree might have played "Viscount Goring" in *An Ideal Husband*, while there is no part in *The Importance of Being Earnest* which could conceivably have interested either actor.

Lane and Rothenstein mentioned are John Lane, the publisher, and Will Rothenstein, the lithographer.

The "proofs" mentioned were probably those for the English edition of *Salomé*. The English translation from the French, in which *Salomé* was originally written, was created by Lord Alfred Douglas.

PAGE 11: [CIRCA 16 APRIL 1894]

The reference to *The Yellow Book* is to the first number of the periodical which was issued in April, 1894.

In the fourth clause of the first sentence of this letter the word "I" has apparently been omitted between the words "and" and "hate," for the sentence should of course run "the gay gilt and gracious lad has gone away and I hate everyone else."

Although Lord Douglas was apparently in Florence when this letter was written, he was absent from London on a journey which took him to Egypt, where he was to have a secretarial position in the diplomatic service, which had been obtained for him by his family in their efforts to separate him from Wilde. He did not, however, remain long away from London. It was at this time that Lord Douglas made the acquaintance of Robert Hitchens which resulted rather unpleasantly for both Wilde and Douglas in Hitchen's book, *The Green Carnation*, satirizing their relationship.

PAGE 12: [CIRCA 20 APRIL 1894]
This letter was written in April, 1894, as is shown by the reference to "Max on Cosmetics," an essay by Max Beerbohm which appeared in the first number of *The Yellow Book*.

Apparently Mansfield was not interested in the idea of Wilde's projected play, *The Cardinal of Avignon*, for the writing never progressed beyond an outline or scenario which was made at this time—April, 1894.

Edward Shelley was a young man employed in the office of Wilde's publishers, with whom Wilde was friendly, and who was later to be one of the Crown's chief witnesses in the criminal section brought against him in May, 1895. The "betrayal" of which Wilde writes, probably alludes to a violent quarrel which had occurred in March, 1993, when Shelley had written a rather bitter letter to Wilde terminating their friendship. (The Trial of Oscar Wilde [1906], p. 94 et seq.)

PAGE 13: [CIRCA JULY 1894]
The reference to "flannels and straw hats" would indicate the coming of warm weather in Paris.

The tone of the letter would seem to indicate more than a casual separation between Lord Alfred Douglas and Oscar Wilde, and follows along quite naturally with the two preceding letters written to Douglas while he was in Italy.

Wilde dedicated *A Woman of No Importance* to Gladys de Grey, who is mentioned in this letter. She became the Marchioness of Ripon in 1909 (Mason Bibliography [1914], p. 402).

"Reggie" is probably Reginald Cholmondeley, mentioned in a later letter written from Dieppe in 1897.

PAGE 15: [JULY–AUGUST 1894]
The reference to Wilde's impending departure for Worthing places the date of this letter in the early summer of 1894. Wilde passed the summer and early autumn of 1894 at this seaside resort near Brighton.

PAGE 17: [AUGUST 1894]
This is obviously the first letter, among the present collection, written after Wilde's arrival at Worthing in the summer of 1894.

Cyril and Vivian were Wilde's two sons. Vivian is now Wilde's literary executor. Cyril was killed in the World War.

PAGE 18: [13 AUGUST 1894]
From its heading and contents, this letter belongs to those written from Worthing during the summer of 1894. The new play referred to is, in all probability, *The Importance of Being Earnest*.

PAGE 20: [8 SEPTEMBER 1894]
The money which Wilde speaks of having received from George Alexander may have been an advance royalty on *The Importance of Being Earnest*, which was produced by Alexander the following February.

PAGE 22: [5 OR 6 NOVEMBER 1894]

This letter was probably written in November 1894. This is deduced from the reference to Wilde's announced intention to attend on Thursday night, "first night" of a new play to be produced by Beerbohm Tree. The year is obviously 1894, as reference is made to the "Scarlet Marquis" divorce which occurred in that year. During 1894, Beerbohm Tree had two "first nights" which fell each on a Thursday. The first was that of Robert Buchanan's play, *The Charlatan*, on Thursday, January 18, and the second that of Haddon Chamber's play, *John-O-Dreams*, on Thursday, November 8. (See "The Theatrical World for 1894," by William Archer.) It is very doubtful if Wilde would have bothered with a play by the bombastic Buchanan, while the next letter in this collection shows that he had been to a play by Haddon Chambers.

"The Scarlet Marquis" was Wilde's deprecatory appellation for Lord Douglas's father, the Marquess of Queensberry.

The divorce referred to was the Marquess's second. After his separation from Lord Alfred's mother in 1889, he was married in 1893 to a Miss Ethel Weedon, from whom he was divorced in 1894.

PAGE 24: [CIRCA 9 NOVEMBER 1894]

This letter should be assigned to November, 1894. The year is quite surely 1894, as is evidenced by reference to worry over money matters, a refrain which runs almost without exception in the letters of 1894, but which does not appear earlier owing presumably to the financial success of *A Woman of No Importance,* in 1893. During 1894, Chambers had two plays produced. One was called *The Fatal Lord*, an Adelphi melodrama, which was produced in September, the other, *John-O-Dreams*, of different character and style and spoken of by critics as a work of considerable importance and style, appeared in November. It does not seem probable that Wilde would have been attracted to the opening of the former play. If we assume that reference in this letter is to the Haddon Chambers play, *John-O-Dreams*, this letter dove-tails perfectly with the preceding one.

PAGE 25: [CIRCA 17 FEBRUARY 1895]
The incident related in the letter and prominently mentioned in most of the Wilde biographies, occurred on the first night of the production of *The Importance of Being Earnest*, at St. James Theatre on February 14, 1895.

The "grotesque bouquet" was one made up of turnips and carrots.

The Percy referred to was probably Lord Alfred Douglas's older brother, who remained sufficiently sympathetic with Douglas and with Wilde to be one of the two sureties of the latter's bond, when Wilde was released on bail after the jury had failed to agree in his first trial.

Douglas was evidently abroad when this letter was written but was apparently hurrying back to London in compliance with Wilde's telegram.

PAGE 33: [2 JUNE 1897]
This letter was written about June 1, after the appearance of an interview with Lord Douglas which was published in *Le Jour* on May 28, 29, or 30, 1897, and before the date of the letter following this on or about June 3, 1897.

This and all subsequent letters herewith published were written within a period of about three months immediately after Wilde's release from Reading Gaol.

On the day of his release, May 19, 1897, Wilde crossed the Channel to France and settled in the little seaside town of Berneval-Sur-Mer, a few miles outside of Dieppe. He assumed the name of M. Sebastian Melmoth, and a number of his friends visited him during the summer. About a month after his arrival, Wilde was housed in the Chalet Bourgeat, which he had remodeled to his needs and here he began writing "The Ballad of Reading Gaol." He continued at this intermittently throughout the summer. The work was interrupted by a visit to Rouen to meet Douglas, because it had seemed imprudent for him to visit Wilde at Berneval. Wilde returned to Berneval and to the poem. But he was restless and unhappy and by October he had joined Lord Douglas in Naples.

It is amusing, if not important, to note that throughout these letters Wilde spells the name of the town in which he was living "Bernaval," which is at variance with the spelling used by his biographers and by Baedeker.

Lugné-Poe, mentioned in this letter, is the French actor M. A.-F. Lugné-Poe, the Director of the Théatre de L'Oeuvre in Paris, and interpreter of the role of Herod when *Salomé* was first produced at that theatre, February 11, 1896, while Wilde was still in prison.

During the time that Wilde was in Reading Gaol, he had in mind two new plays similar in kind to *Salomé*-*Pharaoh* and *Ohab and Isobel*. In this letter he probably refers to plans for the future production of one or the other of these. The plays themselves were never written.

André Gide is the nineteenth-century French author who published a critical essay on the man and his work.

PAGE 37: [3 JUNE 1897]
The Conder and Dal Young referred to are Charles Conder and Dalhousie Young, both well known among the painters, poets, and literateurs of the Eighteen-Nineties. Young was the author of the *Apologia pro Oscar Wilde*, published within a month or two after Wilde's convictions [in 1895].

PAGE 40: 6 JUNE [1897]
The *Chronicle* letter to which Wilde refers was his letter of protest, published in the *Daily Chronicle* in London, May 28, 1897, against

the dismissal of J. Martin, a Warden of Reading Gaol, "for having given some sweet biscuits to a little hungry child." Martin had been an official of Reading Gaol during Wilde's imprisonment and had rendered him numerous friendly services.

PAGE 42: 15 JUNE [1897]
The "Robbie" referred to herein is Robert Ross, Wilde's friend and sometime literary executor.

PAGE 46: 17 JUNE [1897]
It would seem that Wilde's friends, who were anxious to do every-thing possible to prevent the renewal of the intimacy between Wilde and Lord Alfred, had heard of the latter's impending visit to Berneval, and had sent word across the channel which called forth the letter from Wilde's solicitor.

PAGE 48: JUNE 23 [1897]
The fête which Wilde gave the Berneval gamins was, of course, in celebration of the sixtieth anniversary of Queen Victoria's reign.

PAGE 52: [CIRCA 31 AUGUST 1897]
It is uncertain on what date Wilde left for Naples to join Lord Douglas, but he arrived there by October. The meeting with Douglas at Rouen, to which Wilde refers, took place at the end of July, or the first of August. This letter is interesting in view of the denial which it implies to the assertion made by most of his biographers that Wilde returned to Lord Douglas only after the latter's reiterated pleading.

The pleading here most certainly comes from Wilde, and it would be difficult to imagine a more direct or moving appeal to Lord Douglas to resume their life together. But no matter with whom the initiative lay, Wilde left Berneval shortly after writing this letter and joined Lord Douglas in Naples.

AFTERWORD
by Ulrich Baer

Is EXPRESSING YOUR love always honorable and good? How can we tell whether love is real?

Oscar Wilde, today a patron saint for queer love but in his time vilified and imprisoned for his attraction to men by the society which had first celebrated the Irish writer's wit and genius, wrote: "When you really want love, you will find it waiting for you." Did Wilde find love? Central to this question is Wilde's relationship with Lord Alfred Douglas, whom he first met in 1891 when Douglas, nicknamed "Bosie" by his mother, was a twenty-one-year-old student at the University of Oxford and Wilde the widely celebrated author of *The Picture of Dorian Gray* (1890), *The Happy Prince and Other Tales* (1888), and several plays; and also the married father of two young boys. The nature of Wilde and Douglas's relationship has been the subject of countless biographies, several versions of Douglas's memoirs, and adaptations for stage and screen.[1] It also featured prominently in the 1895

---

1 Among biographies of Wilde, these are particularly useful: Richard Ellmann, *Oscar Wilde* (New York: Alfred A. Knopf, 1988); Neil McKenna, *The Secret Life of Oscar Wilde* (New York: Basic Books, 2005); Michele Mendelsohn, *Making Oscar Wilde* (New York: Oxford University Press, 2014); David M. Friedman, *Wilde in America: Oscar Wilde and the Invention of Modern Celebrity* (New York: Norton, 2014); Nicholas Frankel, *Oscar Wilde: The Unrepentant Years* (Cambridge: Harvard University Press,

trials that put Wilde in prison, the first of which was initiated by Wilde against a libelous statement by Douglas's father, and in other trials initiated by Douglas after Wilde's death in 1900. Many of Wilde's biographers ultimately take sides when trying to describe the true nature of Wilde and Bosie's relationship. Did Wilde lose his mind over a younger man, or did this relationship reveal his truth? Did Bosie manipulate Wilde to recklessly initiate a risky trial to take revenge on his estranged father? Did Bosie betray his lover in life through his behavior, and in death via various self-justifying books and libel suits against other Wilde biographers? Did Wilde turn on Bosie in prison, as parts of *De Profundis*, the long essay posing as a letter to Bosie, suggest to some readers? If Wilde had concluded with Bosie while in prison, why did they revive the relationship, again at great risk, after his release?

The first trial had been brought by Wilde against Bosie's father, the Marquess of Queensberry, who, after unsuccessfully trying to confront Wilde in person at London's Albemarle Club (of which Wilde was a member), had left a calling card with the club's porter, inscribed: "For Oscar Wilde, posing Somdomite [*sic*]." But near that trial's end, which Wilde for a while was favored to win via his eloquent defense of homosexuality as a nobler and sublimated "form of affection" than straight love, the prosecutor suddenly threatened to put several rent boys on the stand to testify that they had had sex with Wilde. Wilde instantly accepted a ruling that exonerated Queensberry and ruled his accusation of Wilde "true in substance and in fact."

But here Wilde's real trouble began. Although the first trial had concluded, Wilde was now charged with "sodomy and gross indecency." He had several hours to escape the Crown's jurisdiction before getting arrested, but in a gesture of defiance, pride, or

2017); Matthew Sturgis, *Oscar: A Life* (London: Apollo, 2018).

perhaps foolishness, he stayed put instead of leaving for France. Police seized him. The second trial ended in a hung jury, but in a third trial, Wilde was sentenced to two years' hard labor. After serving his term, the greatest playwright in the English language since William Shakespeare was broke and had few friends left among the cultured crowd in London, whom he had regaled and satirized with brilliant plays and a scandalous novel, *The Picture of Dorian Gray*. To escape the scandal's devastation for the family, his wife Constance Lloyd changed her name to Holland and left England with their two sons, Cyril and Vyvyan, for Switzerland; Wilde would not see the boys again. After his prison term, in 1897, Wilde left for exile in France. To access funds, Wilde consented never to see Bosie again, but quickly broke that promise. Under the assumed name Sebastian Melmoth, Wilde tried to rehabilitate his life for three difficult but "unrepentant" years, as biographer Nicholas Frankel has explained, until succumbing to meningitis at age forty-six.

During Wilde's trials, the Crown put not only homosexuality on the stand but also literature itself. With the guilty verdict, Wilde was condemned by much of English society not only for his deeds but also for his ideas. Although his highly entertaining plays could be mistaken for quick-witted social satires, they examine neither trifles nor the hypocrisy of social conventions but heart-shattering truths of love, loyalty, and integrity. Indeed, Wilde believed social conventions to be vitally important for a functioning society, which is why he eviscerated them with such unremitting intelligence and also wit. The trial turned Wilde into a social martyr and, over the course of a century, into an icon of gay rights. But the trials reveal more than the social mores of late nineteenth-century England. The trials also condemned a person's right to imagine life to be different and not only Wilde's behavior. He was declared guilty of "gross indecency and sodomy," but we do well to understand "gross indecency" to refer not only to homosexuality but to the scandal of imagining life beyond terms society defines as "decent," which means fitting to one's social station. In Wilde's case, he outraged English sensibilities by consorting with working-class men, in keeping with the pro-to-anarchist views that balance the radical individualism typified by his dandy pose with social transformation in his 1891 essay, "The Soul of Man Under Socialism."[2] At the trial's conclusion, the judge expressed outrage at not being able to punish Wilde even more harshly: "It is the worst case I have ever tried. [...] I shall [...] pass the severest sentence that the law allows. In my judgment it is totally inadequate for a case such as this [...] that each of you be imprisoned and kept to hard labor for two years."[3] The judge's rage stems also from his realization that imaginative literature challenges the state's authority not only to shape but also define, and by this act of definition, control, our lives. Once we recognize that Wilde was punished not only for his deeds but also for describing life in terms different from those sanctioned by powerful institutions, we can read his words today without foregone conclusions. Wilde would have rejected the identity of a gay martyr, just as he rejected various other labels on his path from Dublin to world fame. We have only the surviving letters to glimpse a truth about him and Bosie. Taking sides about the relationship, which according to one of Wilde's biographers "pro-vides an example of berserk passion," cuts off what these letters can do for us.[4] They present us with the efforts of two individuals

2   See Kristian Williams, *Resist Everything Except Temptation: The Anarchist Philosophy of Oscar Wilde* (Chico and Edinburgh: AK Press, 2020).

3   H. Montgomery Hyde, *The Trials of Oscar Wilde* (New York: Dover, 1973).

4   Richard Ellmann, "Epilogue," *Oscar Wilde* (New York: Vintage, 1984).

to be transparent and unreservedly honest with one another, fully aware that embarking on this effort without fear or hope may be the hardest thing we can do.

Instead of forcing us to side with either Wilde or Douglas, the surviving correspondence opens up a more general question about the nature of love that transcends their particular relationship, the meaning of which for each of them we can never know. When the story of Wilde and Bosie is distilled to this fundamental question, their relationship resonates beyond Wilde's pivotal role in transforming the social and political attitudes about homosexuality in Western modernity. For this is a question we all harbor, regardless of personal preferences, social circumstances, sexual identities, and political contexts, even when we are blissfully in love: is it real? Tucked in this question, like a tiny jewel lost in bedsheets or a shaggy rug, is another query: does love last?

How to answer this question? How do we lay to rest the doubt that can only be silenced or satisfied by the assurances of another? How do we acknowledge the strange fact that love cannot be proven by means of scientific methods, and yet leaves so much evidence of its existence? Real love must never demand absolute proof. Once we demand proof of another's love, we have left that immanent realm where the other's declaration of love, rather than any action or object, is proof in itself. As the writer Roland Barthes reminds us, declaring one's love expects as its answer a tautology: "I love you" is hoped to be met with another "I love you," and not with the demand to prove one's love. We can read Wilde's letters to Bosie in this spirit: not as psychological, legal, or political evidence—which tracks Wilde's transformation from martyr to icon—but as a reminder that love can never be subsumed into a series of transactions, no matter how complex or sublime.

Ironically, the publication history of Wilde's correspondence with Bosie is largely (though not entirely) transactional. Most of Wilde's surviving letters to Douglas were sold at auction in 1920 in New York City, where bookseller A. S. W. Rosenbach bought them at considerable cost and then resold them to philanthropist William Andrews Clark Jr. Clark, who in collaboration with Rosenbach, published his prized possession soon thereafter as *Some Letters from Oscar Wilde to Alfred Douglas, 1892–1897*, with an essay by Rosenbach and edited by Arthur C. Dennison Jr. and Harrison Post, in San Francisco in 1924. Clark, the founder of the Los Angeles Philharmonic, was a great bibliophile who ultimately bequeathed his own collection of books to the Southern Branch of the University of California (today's UCLA), where it became part of the William Andrews Clark Memorial Library. Today, the Clark Library holds the largest collection of materials related to Wilde anywhere. This would have pleased Wilde, who during his 1882–83 lecture tour of the United States said: "No part of America has struck me so favorably as California," and later added, in an acquaintance's remembrance, that the American West was "where a man can be a man today, and yesterdays don't count."[5] Of the two hundred and twenty-five original copies of *Some Letters from Oscar Wilde to Alfred Douglas, 1892–1897*, a few dozen copies survive in rare book collections in the United States, with several additional copies in the United Kingdom, Ireland, and Canada.

But this story of high-priced book sales, a legendary bookseller, a wealthy American collector, and a provocative 1924 privately printed, limited edition of Wilde's letters has one feature that is not merely transactional. The explicit intent of the edition was to correct the one-sided record created by Wilde himself in the book-long autobiographical text written in prison, later

---

5 Bernhard Thornton, "Oscar Wilde–A Reminiscence," *Theatre Magazine*, volume 27 (1918).

named *De Profundis*.[6] That text had been addressed to Douglas, but was given to someone else. But *De Profundis* is not a letter but an autobiographical text running to 50,000 words. In that text Wilde tried to make sense of himself to himself, rather than make himself be present to another, as he does in his letters to Bosie. In 1905, five years after Wilde's death, parts of *De Profundis* were published by Robert Ross, one of Wilde's former lovers and Bosie's rival. Wilde had stipulated that the full manuscript should remain in the British Library and not be made accessible until 1960. But additional parts of *De Profundis* were read out in a court case as evidence in a trial involving Douglas in 1913. (The complete text finally appeared in unexpurgated form in 1962.) The 1924 slim volume of Wilde's letters that forms the basis of this volume is an effort to correct Wilde's own account of Bosie's role in his life. Wilde's actions, especially his decision to rejoin Bosie in France, and the letters he wrote to Douglas after his discharge from prison contradict the impression *De Profundis* gives. The letters are in keeping with the spirit of Wilde, who preferred inconsistency to predictable behavior and valued the idea of personality far more than the static notion of "character."

But in addition to its stated purpose of correcting a misperception of Wilde's biography generated by Wilde himself—and also by various biographers, former lovers, Douglas, and court transcripts—the 1924 publication presents, in itself, a somewhat perplexing message for future generations. Strangely, and without a real explanation, Clark and Rosenbach decided to include in their edition of Wilde's letters a letter by Lord Alfred Douglas. This letter was written at a crucial moment in Wilde's life: while he was awaiting the sentence of hard labor in the trial

---

6   Colm Tóibín, "Introduction," in: *Oscar Wilde, De Profundis and Other Prison Writings*, edited and with an introduction by Colm Tóibín (New York: Penguin, 2013).

that would put him into prison for two years. Douglas's letter had appeared in facsimile in a limited-edition biography written by Wilde's friend Frank Harris in 1910, *Oscar Wilde: His Life and Confessions*. Clark and Rosenbach decided also to include it only in facsimile, which underlines its unclear status in that volume and separates it visually and metaphorically from Wilde's correspondence.

Why did Clark and Rosenbach include Bosie's testimony of his love written at a moment when Wilde was being abandoned by most of his friends, family, associates, and admirers socially or legally defined?

Rosenbach achieved enormous fame, notoriety, and great wealth as "Dr. R." in the 1920s and '30s rare-book trade, when he was also nicknamed "the Terror of the Auction Room" and the "Napoleon of Books." He is assumed to have traded books valued at \$75 million in today's money. His personal collection, including the manuscript of James Joyce's *Ulysses* (1920) and Bram Stoker's notes for *Dracula* (1897), is held today at the revered Rosenbach Museum and Library in Philadelphia. Abraham S. W. Rosenbach and his older brother Philip were colorful characters, who kept live terrapin, ready for supper, in the basement of their town house and sold and bought enormously valuable books, especially early American literature not yet favored by America's wealthy classes. These are now housed in major collections, including the Folger Library, the Morgan Library and Museum in New York City, and the Clark Library at UCLA.

There is precious little information about A. S. W. Rosenbach's private life. In scholarly essays, he is called "a life-long bachelor" who died of the effects of an "unrestrained life." His single foray into fiction, the intriguingly titled *The Unpublishable Memoirs* (1917), concludes with the tale of a roguish book dealer who tricks rich people out of their printed treasures and marries not for love but to obtain a rare book; the final pages are a diatribe against marriage. It's hard not to call a book in which the wife leaves her protagonist husband because of his "wicked, unnatural, unspeakable" love for books, which finally allows him to indulge in his "real" passion from now on, queer. The Rosenbach Library's website stresses that "*The Unpublishable Memoirs* is not a personal memoir, but a work of fiction"; Rosenbach's biography describes the book as "his farewell gesture to a former way of life" of a literary writer.[7] But Rosenbach's essay in *Some Letters from Oscar Wilde to Alfred Douglas, 1892–1897* seems missing from existing biographical accounts. At the 1920 New York auction, Rosenbach had bought twenty-five of Wilde's letters for $7,900 ($103,000 in today's money), with other Wilde manuscripts for a total of $44,881 ($590,000 in today's money). Rosenbach and Clark treasured Wilde's letters as much for literary merit as for their author's notoriety; in a 1936 essay reprinted in this volume, "Letters That We Ought to Burn," Rosenbach empathizes with "Wilde's despair" at seeing the poet John Keats's love letters for sale at auction in 1885, but notes, with his trademark irony, that Wilde was "little dreaming that [...] his own letters [...] would appear on the auction block [...] and be published for the delectation of a naughty world." Rosenbach does not mention in that essay that he himself had published Wilde's letters, as a key operator in the "naughty world." He mentions only his purchase of the manuscript of Wilde's 1886 sonnet "On the Sale by Auction of Keats' Love Letters" (today housed in the Rosenbach's collection in Philadelphia). Many of Wilde's letters were destroyed by their recipients after the author went to jail, fearing incrimination; and Wilde's son, Vyvyan Holland, had censored most letters that were published before the 1950s. Why did Rosenbach include and draw attention to Bosie's letter in the small, private 1924 printing

---

7   Edwin Wolf, *A. S. W. Rosenbach: A Biography* (Philadelphia: World Publishing Company, 1960).

of Wilde's letters, only available in the United States at the time?

Here is Rosenbach's explanation for including the facsimile of Bosie's letter:

> There is included in Mr. Clark's collection a single letter written by Lord Alfred Douglas to Oscar Wilde. This is given without comment at the end of the volume. As has been stated before the letters are terribly human. They begin so debonair, so gracious and so winning. Alas! They end so differently. The tragedy of Wilde's life ebbs and flows through them. The very qualities of the writer are revealed to us as in a mirror. It is for this reason that they are now given to the world.

Wilde, like his precursor Shakespeare and his contemporary Friedrich Nietzsche, valued masks more than displaying one's authentic self. In 1886, he published an essay ostensibly on costumes in Shakespeare performances titled "The Truth of Masks: A Note on Illusion," which ends with the quasi-Nietzschean declaration, perhaps also shared by Wilde's contemporary, the American poet Walt Whitman: "Not that I agree with everything that I have said in this essay. There is much with which I entirely disagree."[8] Writing, for Wilde, has not only the purpose of revealing a single truth, but aims for various effects, just as love letters do not *prove* the writer's love but, if they hit their mark, have an effect on the recipient.

Wilde was punished harshly when one mask was ripped off during his trials with the aim of revealing his true nature, in

---

8   Oscar Wilde, "The Truth of Masks," in: Wilde, *Intentions* (London: Methuen, 1891); republished in: *The Complete Works of Oscar Wilde IV: Criticism: Historical Criticism, Intentions, The Soul of Man*, ed. by Josephine M. Guy (Oxford: Oxford University Press, 2007).

the prosecutor's understanding of that idea. But for Wilde, the search for a person's "true nature" goes against his understanding of human nature itself, which is malleable or, in contemporary parlance, performative. Rosenbach's essay about Wilde's letters to Bosie also lifts a mask, but rather than revealing a hidden truth it creates a particular mood. Rosenbach noted that through Wilde's letters, the "very qualities of the writer are revealed to us as in a mirror." But what is revealed to us in Bosie's letter? To me, the letter says that Wilde and Bosie's love was real when Bosie wrote the letter, and it was real when Wilde received it—even if Bosie later hedged on the nature of their bond. This is so because love letters do not only communicate intense feelings, but seek to manifest and invoke the lover to the letter's recipient. In this sense, love letters do not communicate anything but the fact that they have been written and something about the atmosphere in that moment. But the letter also holds a mirror up to Rosenbach, who drew attention to its inclusion "without comment."

What can Bosie's love letter to Wilde mean to us today, when gay marriage has been legal in the United Kingdom since 2014, and in the United States since 2015, and Wilde's plays are read by high school students everywhere, while he had been imprisoned for "corrupting" the young? Victorian London jeered, shamed, and imprisoned Wilde. It took British officials 122 years to pardon him, in a 2017 blanket ruling dubbed "Alan Turing Law," named for computer scientist Alan Turing (1912–1954) following Turing's posthumous pardon in 2013 of a 1952 conviction for "gross indecency" which Turing fulfilled by undergoing chemical castration.

What did Bosie's letter mean to Wilde? We know that they resumed their relationship after his prison term, even if passages in Wilde's *De Profundis* accuse Bosie of excessive vanity and have, for this reason, been interpreted as Wilde's renunciation of his former lover. Does Bosie's letter outweigh *De Profundis* and reveal the truth of their relationship?

Lord Alfred Douglas's letter to Oscar Wilde is brought to us, and now resides in rare book collections, thanks to A. S. W. Rosenbach's stature and influence. But perhaps Rosenbach commented specifically on Douglas's letter to partly lift his mask and signal something not mentioned by his biographers. In the spot habitually reserved for the names of spouses and descendants, Rosenbach's rightly effusive *New York Times* obituary in 1952 concludes with the deflating line: "His clubs were the Grolier in New York, and the Philobiblon [*sic*] in Philadelphia." Perhaps Bosie's letter allowed Rosenbach to speak to future readers what he would not communicate to his contemporaries in his words. This makes me think of Bosie's letter as a work of literature, posing a question for us today about the reality of love, rather than fodder for another biography. Bosie's letter bears witness to the fact that expressing one's love remains an act of courage in any age.

A BIBLIOGRAPHICAL PREFACE
by William Andrews Clark, Jr.

THE LAMENTABLE HISTORY of Oscar O'Flahertie Wills Wilde, after his release from incarceration in Wandsworth prison and in Reading Gaol, has been related in the standard biographies of his life, such as, among others, those by Robert H. Sherard, Arthur Ramsone, Leonard Creswell Ingleby, and Frank Harris. These authors were well acquainted with the facts and the details of Wilde's life up to the time of his death in dire poverty in Paris at the sordid Hôtel D'Alsace, rue des Beaux-Arts, in November 1900.

The closing history in the poet's life has been further augmented and additional light thrown in perspective upon his activities of this period by books that have recently come from the presses of England and of America, namely: In England—*After Reading,* London, March 12, 1921, Beaumont Press; *After Berneval,* London, February 20, 1922, Beaumont Press; limited to 475 copies of which were printed on Japanese vellum. And in America—*Letters After Reading, I. Berneval,* New York, April 8, 1921, Paul R. Reynolds, and *Letters After Reading, II. Naples and Paris,* New York December 31, 1921, Paul R. Reynolds.

The letters contained in these volumes are all addressed to Robert Ross and the contents of the books are described in my library catalog of Wilde and Wildeiana, Vol. II (1922), pp. 3–5; wherein I remarked that "these letters are particularly interesting in that they trace the gradual evolution of the "Ballad of Reading Gaol"; that they contained "drafts of verses with the poet's comments on and the reasons for the phraseology employed."

From the student's point of view the letters are of stupendous interest as showing Wilde's extraordinary personality, his artistry, and his development in ever increasing strength as a master of English style and prose and in verse.

A few years ago I bought at private sale twenty-five letters written by Oscar Wilde to Lord Alfred Douglas, from various places on the Continent, after he had left England never again to return. These letters were sold at auction at the Anderson Galleries, New York, April 23, 1920, when the library of John B. Stetson, Jr., was dispersed. They have never before been published and it is alone through the kindness of Mr. Vyvyan Holland, Wilde's literary executor, that they now appear for the first time.

The epistles speak for themselves. They are most intimate in character, but as Dr. Rosenbach has said in his masterly essay to this volume, they should belong to the world.

Mr. John Henry Nash, in his usual artistic style has reproduced the text of the letters in the Caslan Oldstyle type, on Deckle D'Aigle paper made in America. The letters, too, are reproduced in facsimile on Alexandra Japan, likewise of American make. The facsimiles are printed directly from copperplates.

The frontispiece is a reproduction in photogravure from an autographed cabinet size photograph now in my library. "Bosie," that appears thereon, was Wilde's pet name for Lord Alfred Douglas. It is dated 1894, and if taken of him in that year he was twenty-four years of age at that time.

Wilde's calligraphy as noted in his early letters was large, clear and youthful. In his middle period it was neat and tiny, but his last letters were written in an almost illegible flowing scrawl.

The task of unraveling the letters, that appear in this volume in facsimile, I assigned to Mr. Arthur C. Dennison, Jr., and to Mr. Harrison Post, one of my assistant librarians. Mr. Dennison, I regret to say, but a few months ago was lost at sea on his way to Cuba. Theirs was no easy task, as the facsimiles themselves show. Wilde often used stenographic characters in place of the written word. After the letters had been translated as it were, Messrs. Dennison and Post collaborated in assembling the notes to the letters, which appear in the text preceding the facsimiles.

Here, too, much difficulty was encountered by them, for the reason that Wilde seldom dated any of his letters, and it required on the part of these collaborators much research work and reading of biographies in order to co-ordinate the facts which they gathered with the context of each separate letter, so as to arrive at the chronological sequence in which the letters should be placed. I have followed their notes in placing the letters as they appear in this volume and I desire herewith to give them all credit for a splendid piece of work, enthusiastically performed.

Included in this volume and at the end thereof I have placed a facsimile of a letter written, dated 15th day of May, 1895, from Hotel des Deux Mondes, Paris, by Lord Alfred Douglas to Oscar Wilde, wherein the former addresses the latter as "My darling Oscar." This letter does not properly belong to the collection that I bought a private sale as heretofore mentioned. It is, however, of so great interest relative to their friendship that, together with this fact, and because Dr. Rosenbach mentions it in this essay, I concluded to make use thereof. The original of this letter is in my private collection.

It has already appeared in facsimile in the limited edition of *The Life of Oscar Wilde,* by Frank Harris.

In putting out this volume, I owe a great debt to many too numerous to mention, whose co-operation I fully appreciate and acknowledge herewith.

Los Angeles, California, July, 1924

AN ESSAY
by A. S. W. Rosenbach

No ONE HAS been praised so much and damned more heartily than Oscar Wilde. It has been said he was one of the most brilliant talkers that ever lived, but he had no Boswell to place imperishably before the world the many charming sallies of his wit. Lord Alfred Douglas, in the beautiful sonnet, *The Dead Poet*, alludes feelingly to these now-buried graces:

> And then methought outside a fast locked gate
> I mourned the loss of unrecorded words,
> Forgotten tales and mysteries half said
> Wonders that might have been articulate.

Nowhere was Wilde so glorious, so naïve, and so impulsive as in his letters. In his books we see the calm, thoughtful, retrospective artist, who, although playful, even joyous at times, was always reserved, classic in his manner, in fact, the "lord of language." It was in the Comedy of Manners that Wilde excelled; this was the medium in which he could best display his sparkling, although never caustic wit, the exuberance of his humor, the brilliance of his epigraphs, the ever-compelling flow of his spirits.

Oscar Wilde, although a master of the lighter comedy, the equal of Congreve and Wycherley, could never in his writings touch the tragic note. This was apart from his nature and anguish and despair could not command his pen. He tried in *Salomé* and *The Picture of Dorian Gray*, but the attempt was a failure, without sincerity and without truth. He could write of the joys of earth and the ecstasies of Heaven, but he never succeeded in picturing the soul-agonies of the lost or the bitter cup of the damned.

Quite unconsciously, however, Oscar Wilde has given us a picture of his own sorrows, of his wrecked life that is almost without a parallel in literary history. It is in his letters to Lord Alfred Douglas, now printed for the first time, that his nakedness is exhibited to use frankly almost indecently, and there is nothing in them that can cover or shield him.

It is not for this reason that the letters are revealed to the world. They are now issued in order to give a truer impression of the man and his life than we formerly possessed. For in *De Profundis* Oscar Wilde deliberately set to work to create a wrong impression. In the silence of Reading Gaol he used his pen with merciless effect. He wrote cruelly, critically, with his tongue in his cheek. He thought he had eons of time before him, as his two years' sentence appeared to him, and in the dock of his prison he weaved his story, polished and embellished it, embroidering his tale with the witchery of style and language.

It is on account of this that *De Profundis* is not a truthful human document. It is full of lies, deceit, honeyed phrases, and mock religion. In the letters to Alfred Douglas, dashed off quickly, without a moment's thought that they would be seen by other eyes, there is nothing that is not self-revealing.

When *De Profundis* was first published in 1905 everyone had the impression that it was a complete retrospect addressed to Robert Ross. We know now that it was a long letter to Lord Alfred Douglas and that Robert Ross merely pieced together the parts he designed to give to the world; the most interesting portion he consigned to the Trustees of the British Museum with instructions that the manuscript was not to be unsealed until 1960. A few years ago as a result of the suit brought by Douglas against Arthur Ransome, the judge ordered that it be produced in court and thus the entire letter was revealed to the curious. In 1913 fifteen copies were privately printed in New York to secure the American copyright. It was entitled *The Suppressed Portion of De Profundis Now for the First Time published by his Literary Executor, Robert Ross, New York, Paul R. Reynolds, 1913.*

Lord Alfred Douglas, in his *Oscar Wilde and Myself,* denounces Ross for publishing *De Profundis* in the mutilated way in which we all know it best. We quite agree with him. In it Wilde appears transmuted into a different, if not a purer being. In the twenty-five letters contained herein Wilde stands forth in his true and proper colors revealed unsparingly to the world. It is also entirely different from the tinctured version given by Douglas in his book, which is unworthy of a friend and inexcusable in an enemy.

There were some grounds for writing about Douglas in the strain Wilde attempted in *De Profundis.* In the silence of his prison tomb hardly a word came from the man for whom Wilde thought he sacrificed so much. In order to understand the story it is necessary to give a brief resumé gathered from the lips of the two actors in this tragic show. Frank Harris has admirably told the tale, but we prefer to give it here from their own correspondence.

The letters disclose the fact that Wilde met Lord Alfred Douglas while he was an undergraduate at Oxford. Douglas had already given his ear to the Muse of Poetry and was editor of the *Spirit Lamp,* a college magazine. The letters of this period seem trivial, light, fanciful, and written in that jeweled, artificial style that Wilde used so effectively in *Dorian Gray.* Even at this era, from 1892 on, the letters are curiously self-revealing. They give a wonderful picture of Wilde at the height of his power and of his popularity.

The time of the action of this tragedy, as traced in the letters, is exactly eight years. It follows almost the course of the famous Elizabethan models, and the unfolding of the plot is just as seductive and absorbing. For in these brief years Oscar Wilde reached the pinnacle of his greatness, and one can watch, as in a box at the play, the stalking figure of Nemesis first tempt and then destroy. We must, however, pass quickly over the first portion of the play and hasten to the turning point: Wilde's suit against the Marquis of Queensberry.

It was in Holloway Prison, awaiting trial, that Oscar Wilde turned to his friend. In those anxious days it is true that Douglass called to see him, as the following testifies. From Holloway, November 23, 1895, Wilde thus writes to Mrs. Leverson:

> MY DEAR SPHINX:
> … Today Bosie comes early to see me—my counsel seems to want the case to be tried at once—I don't—nor dear Bosie,—bail, or no bail, I think we had better wait.
>
> I have seen counsel, and Bosie; I don't know what to do—my life seems to have gone from me—I feel caught in a terrible net. I don't know where to turn; I care less when I think that is thinking of me,—I think of nothing else.
>
> OSCAR

The letters from Alfred Douglas suddenly stopped and Wilde was in the throes of despair. He advised Douglas to leave at once for the Continent, which he did, while Wilde remained to face the terrible and scorching fire. No word came from Douglas. Twice in 1895 he wrote to Mrs. Leverson, "I have had no letter as yet today from Fleur-de-lys—I wait with strange hunger for it"—and a few months later, "I have not had a line today from Fleur-de-lys. I suppose he is at Rouen. I am so wretched when I don't hear from him; today I am bored, and sick to the death of imprisonment."

It was in this state of mind, with this feeling of resentment and bitterness in his heart, that Wilde wrote *De Profundis*. The part that Robert Ross saw fit to give to us is a noble fragment, which was read by many with the thought that at least one sinner had been saved; and that a soul had been whitened within the prison walls. Wilde himself wrote, "I feel sure that in elemental forces there is purification and I want to go back to them and live in their presence."

The true *De Profundis*, as it was really written, we know now to be an insidious attack upon the man Wilde termed his friend, the "dear Bosie" of the letters. It seems a pity to denounce a work, which when it appeared gave genuine pleasure to many people. But the truth must out, so we proceed to the second period when Wilde was released from jail and went forth to see again the stars.

In the *vita nuova* far removed from the shadow of prison and of pain, by the sea, which, as Wilde states, "washes away the stains and wounds of the world," this bitterness disappears. In sunny Berneval he again feels the joy of life surging in his veins. It is during this period of freedom that the "Ballad of Reading Gaol" was written. Apart from this and a few short articles his genius was sterile.

The fair words and promises of *De Profundis* were thrown to the winds. Wilde sought in Paris and in Dieppe to reclaim his lost soul, not the one that had been bruised and cleansed in Holloway and Reading, but that Pagan one that was the source of all his suffering. He returned to his former companions and in the life that he denounced in such an extraordinary manner in *De Profundis*. This is set forth vividly in the ensuing letter.

It has been stated by nearly all his biographers and by Wilde himself in prison, that Lord Alfred Douglas was the spirit "tempting him to ill." This, however was far from the truth. He writes to "his own darling boy" from Dieppe that his "only hope of doing beautiful work in art is being with you....do remake my ruined life for me."

Wilde, before his departure for Naples, had written to Douglas, "every one is furious with me for going back to you"; this included his wife, his trustees, and nearly all his friends. Let Oscar Wilde tell his own story in the extracts from unpublished letters written to the Sphinx, Mrs. Leverson, and to his publisher, Mr. Leonard Smithers; and let the reader sit in judgment.

> My Dear Ada,
>
> ...But now, as the absurd income I had—£3 a week, has been stopped by my trustees because I am here with Bosie, the only friend I have who is able or willing to be with me—I am forced to do so—and I find that I cannot get my poem, a long poem of 700 lines, accepted even by the most revolting New York paper. So I am face to face with starvation; not in any theatrical sense, but as an ugly fall; of course, Bosie, as you know, has only £25 a month, and naturally it is not enough for his own wants, he cannot financially help me with either the smallest sum or the most meagre assistance. He simply has not got the money....

Writing from Naples in February, 1898, to Leonard Smithers, he says:

> As I have lost my entire income, of course, I cannot live with Alfred Douglas any more. He has only just enough for himself. So he is going back to Paris and

I will be alone here. I do not know if now that we are going to separate, there is any likelihood of my income being restored to me. I unluckily have now no one to plead my case aright, I have alienated all my friends, partly thru' my own fault, and partly thru' theirs. The Paris Journal has a sympathetic paragraph to say I am staying at Naples—but French people subscribe nothing but sonnets when one is alive and statues when one is not.

Again writing to Smithers about the proposed separation from Douglas, he remarks:

I wish you would start a Society for the Defense of Oppressed personalities: at present there is a gross European Concern headed by brutes and solicitors against us. It is really ridiculous that after my entire life had been wrecked by Society, people should still propose to exercise social tyranny over me, and try to force me to live in solitude,—the one thing I can't stand. I lived in silence and solitude for two years in prison. I did not think that on my release, my wife, my trustees, the guardians of my children, my few friends, such as they are, and my myriad enemies, would combine to force me by starvation to live in silence and solitude again.... The scheme is put forward on moral grounds! It is proposed to leave me to die of starvation, or to blow my brains out in a Naples urinal. I never came across anyone in whom the moral sense was dominant who was not heartless, cruel, vindictive, log-stupid, and completely lacking in the smallest sense of humanity. Moral people as they are termed, are simple beasts. I would sooner have fifty unnatural vices than one unnatural virtue.

These letters speak eloquently. They sum up the situation better than any biographer however just and impartial he may be. It has not been our purpose to defend Douglas in any way. His *Oscar Wilde and Myself*, is supposed by Douglas, and by no one else, to be a defence. It is, however, necessary for us to dispel a mendacious impression, a false atmosphere, that Wilde created many years ago, and which, if not corrected would have crept into the chronicle of our literary history.

There is included in Mr. Clark's collection [of Wilde's letters to Douglas] a single letter written by Lord Alfred Douglas to Oscar Wilde. This is given without comment at the end of the volume.

As has been stated before the letters are terribly human. They begin so debonair, so gracious and so winning. Alas! they end so differently. The tragedy of Wilde's life ebbs and flows through them. The very qualities of the writer are revealed to us as in a mirror. It is for this reason that they are now given to the world.

LETTERS THAT WE OUGHT TO BURN

by A. S. W. Rosenbach

ONE SUMMER AFTERNOON about ten years ago, Arnold Bennett and I were taking tea at a charming old place called The Compleat Angler, at Marlow on the Thames. Bennett had selected a table in the garden above the weir, with a broad view of the river. People floated by lazily in punts. The atmosphere was altogether dreamy and delightful. Suddenly we sat up, all eyes. An extremely beautiful woman was drifting close to the shore.

"You know who she is?" We both spoke at once, then smiled. Of course we knew. So did everyone, if the craning of necks at other tables indicated anything. A fascinating American was this lady. Only a short time before, she had made a laughing-stock of one of the most conservative men in England, a certain Lord X, whose real name I am sure you would recognize if I had the temerity to tell it.

From A. S. W. Rosenbach, *A Book Hunter's Holiday: Adventures with Books and Manuscripts* (Boston and New York: Houghton Mifflin Company, 1936). Used by permission of The Rosenbach, Philadelphia.

Lord X wrote letters to his beautiful friend that were of such an intimate nature that they disclosed a side to his character hitherto entirely unsuspected by his friends. Frankly, they were most amusing even to the casual reader—they were published in the ha'penny press—and I thought them a bit tragic too.

For they revealed what was the passion—his passion—of a lifetime, and in a manner that fitted neither his age nor his background.

I looked at Bennett, whose observant eyes were still on the river.

"What," I asked, "do you believe was the first letter ever written?" "A dun—or a love-letter," he replied quickly.

"Which, really?"

"Most likely a dun," he said in his practical manner, as he buttered a fresh piece of toast. But I shook my head, preferring to keep my few illusions. I thought, and still think, that the first letter ever written was a love-letter.

It was naturally in my youth that I first became interested in love-letters. Yet, thirty years ago, I had an altogether different view from that which I have today. I felt a certain shyness, suffered twinges of conscience reading letters that were only intended for the eyes of one person. To me, it was on a par with peeking through a keyhole. The lines that Shelley wrote to Mary Godwin, or Keats telling the agony of his love to "beautiful and elegant, graceful, silly, fashionable and strange" Fanny Brawne, seemed to me sacred. I understood Oscar Wilde's despair, which caused him to write his exquisite sonnet on the sale at auction of Keats's love-letters to Fanny Brawne. Wilde was present that March 2, 1885, little dreaming that the time would come when his own letters, even the original manuscript of the poem that he penned that very day, would appear on the auction block. Wilde's sonnet runs as follows:

On the Sale by Auction of Keats' Love Letters

These are the letters which Endymion wrote
To one he loved in secret, and apart,
And now the brawlers of the auction mart
Bargain and bid for each poor blotted note,
Ay! For each separate pulse of passion quote
The latest price—I think they love not Art
Who break the crystal of a poet's heart
That small and sickly eyes may glare or gloat.
Is it not said, that many years ago
In a far Eastern town some soldiers ran
With torches through the midnight, and began
To wrangle for mean raiments, and to throw
Dice for the garments of a wretched man,
Not knowing the God's wonder or his woe?

Sonnet.

On the sale by auction of Keats' Love-Letters.

—

These are the letters which Endymion wrote
  To one he loved in secret, and apart,
  And now the brawlers of the auction mart
Bargain and bid for each poor blotted note,
Ay! for each separate pulse of passion quote
  The latest price. — I think they love not Art
  Who break the crystal of a poet's heart
That small and sickly eyes may glare or gloat.

Is it not said, that many years ago
  In a far Eastern town some soldiers ran
  With torches through the midnight, and began
To wrangle for mean raiment, and to throw
  Dice for the garments of a wretched man,
Not knowing the God's wonder or his woe.

                    Oscar Wilde.

March. 1.
    1885.

The manuscript of this famous poem I purchased at a sale in New York in 1920. At the same auction, a letter of John Keats to Fanny Brawne sold for eight hundred dollars, and is now in the remarkable collection of my friend Mr. Carl H. Pforzheimer. It was at this sale that Christopher Morley was inspired to write his beautiful sonnet, "In an Auction Room," which he dedicated to me and I consider finer than Wilde's.

In an Auction Room
Letter of John Keats to Fanny Brawne

Anderson Galleries, March 15, 1920, to Dr. A. S. W. Rosenbach

"How about this lot?" said the auctioneer;
"One hundred, may I say, just for a start?"
Between the plum-red curtains, drawn apart
A written sheet was held.... And strange to hear
(Dealer, would I were steadfast as thou art),
The cold quick bids. (Against you in the rear!)
The crimson salon, in a glow more clear,
Burned bloodlike purple as the poet's heart.

Song that outgrew the singer! Bitter Love
That broke the proud hot heart it held in thrall,
Poor script, where still those tragic passions move,
Eight hundred bid: fair warning: the last call:
The soul of Adonais, like a star....
Sold for eight hundred dollars—Doctor R!

CHRISTOPHER MORLEY

For
A.S.W.R.

GREEN ESCAPE
ROSLYN HEIGHTS
NEW YORK

In an Auction Room

[Letter of John Keats to Fanny Browne -
sold at the Anderson Galleries, March 15, 1920]

How about this lot? said the auctioneer;
One Hundred, may I say, just for a start?
Between the plum-red curtains, drawn apart,
A written sheet was held.... And strange to hear
(Dealer, would I were steadfast as thou art)
The cold quick bids. (Against you in the rear!)
The crimson salon, in a glow more clear
Burned bloodlike purple as the poet's heart.

Song that outgrew the singer! Bitter Love
That broke the proud hot heart it held in thrall —
Poor script, where still those tragic passions move —
Eight Hundred bid: fair warning: the last call:
The soul of Adonais, like a star....
Sold for Eight Hundred Dollars — Doctor R!

Christopher Morley

After having acquired the Wilde sonnet for my own collection, I had to have some of the letters that poor Keats penned to Fanny Brawne. My quest had to be most secretive, for my friend, the late Amy Lowell, was then engaged on her great life of Keats. She would have been furious if I had secured letters and refused to surrender them to her. Three finally came my way; one particularly I coveted. Lord Rosebery purchased it at the original sale in 1885 and would never part with it. At his death I bought it from his daughter, Lady Sybil Grant. Written by the poet to Fanny Brawne just before his departure for Rome—he died there on February 23, 1821—he was torn with jealousy and forebodings:

Wednesday Morn[in]g. [Kentish Town, towards the end of 1820]

MY DEAREST GIRL,

I have been [on] a walk this morning with a book in my hand, but as usual I have been occupied with nothing but you: I wish I could say in an agreeable manner. I am tormented day and night. They talk of my going to Italy. 'Tis certain I shall never recover if I am to be so long separate from you: yet with all this devotion to you I cannot persuade myself into any confidence of you. Past experience connected with the fact of my long separation from you gives me agonies which are scarcely to be talked of. When your mother comes I shall be very sudden and expert in asking her whether you have been to Mrs. Dilke's, for she might say not to make me easy. I am literally worn to death, which seems my only recourse. I cannot forget what has pass'd. What? nothing with a man of the world, but to me dreadful. When you were in the habit of flirting with Brown you would have left off, could your own heart have felt one half of one pang mine did. Brown is a good sort of a Man—he did not know he was doing me to death by inches. I feel the effect of every one of those hours in my side now; and for that cause, though he has done me many services, though I know his love and friendship for me, though at this moment I should be without peace were it not for his assistance, I will never see or speak to him until we are both old men, if we are to be. I will resent my heart having been made a football. You will call this madness. I have heard you say that it was not unpleasant to wait a few years—you have amusements—your mind is away—you have not brooded over one idea as I have, and how should you? You are to me an object intensely desirable—the air I breathe in a room empty of you is unhealthy. I am not the same to you—no—you can wait—you have a thousand activities—you can be happy without me. Any party, anything to fill up the days has been enough. How have you pass'd this month? Whom have you smil'd with? All this may seem savage in me. You do not feel as I do—you do not know what it is to love—one day you may—your time has not come. Ask yourself how many unhappy hours Keats has caused you in Loneliness. For myself I have been a Martyr the whole time, and for this reason I speak; the confession is forc'd from me by the torture. I appeal to you by the blood of that Christ you believe in: Do not write to me if you have done anything this month which it would have pained me to have seen. You may have altered—if you have not—I you still behave in dancing rooms and other societies as I have seen you—I do not want to live—if you have done so I wish this coming night may be my last. I cannot live without you, and not only you but chaste you; virtuous you. The Sun rises and sets, the day passes, and you follow the bent of your inclination to a certain extent—you have no conception of the quantity of miserable feelings that passes through me in a day. Be serious! Love is not a plaything—and again do not write unless you can do it with a crystal conscience. I would sooner die for want of you than—

Yours forever,

J. KEATS

Ten years after the Keats sale, during Oscar Wilde's celebrated trial, someone broke into his attractive little house in Tite Street in London, and made away with many of his manuscripts and letters.

By devious routes they appeared at auction or private sale. I remember my brother Philip telling me that directly after the trial, he went into a famous bookshop in London, looking for manuscripts of Oscar Wilde. Although he asked for them in an ordinary tone, the clerk replied in a whisper, and immediately called the proprietor. Sheepishly they led him into a back room, closing the door tightly. To his surprise, he saw on a table the original drafts of Wilde's three plays, *The Importance of Being Earnest, The Ideal Husband,* and *Lady Windermere's Fan.*

"Why all this mystery?" exclaimed Philip, now thoroughly astonished.

The bookseller behaved as though the room contained contraband. It was obvious that the sooner he got those manuscripts out of his shop, the better he would feel. So my brother bought them immediately, believing that a man's conduct has nothing to do with his genius.

The papers taken from Tite Street included letters from Constance Lloyd Wilde to Oscar, when she was engaged to him.

They are the most heartbreaking letters I have ever read, and bear out my belief that the greatest love-letters are not necessarily written by great people—even, to use Wilde's own phrase, "lords of language." Constance Lloyd had no literary pretensions. Here is an extract from one of her letters:

> MY DARLING LOVE,
>
> I am sorry I was so silly: you take all my strength away, I have no power to do anything but just love you when you are with me.... Every day that I see you, every moment you are with me I worship you more, my whole life is yours to do as you will with it, such a poor gift to offer up to you, but yet all I have and so you will not despise it....Do believe that I love you most passionately with all the strength of my heart and mind: anything that you asked me to do, I would in order to convince you and make you happy.
>
> ...When I have you for my husband, I will hold you fast with chains of love and devotion so that you will never leave me, or love any-one as I can love & comfort you.

Today, I do not feel at all squeamish about reading other persons' love-letters. Of course I refer to those written by celebrities of the past. As a young man, I wasn't alone in considering love-letters sacred to the persons who wrote or received them. Biographers were very much of that opinion, too. Perhaps that explains why there were so many dull biographies published in the early nineteen-hundreds. The truth is, love-letters show men and women as they really are. Today, one of the first things an author does, in planning a biography, is to locate the love-letters written by the person he is portraying. So, you see, collecting these letters is a matter of historical interest, not merely prying into the secret affairs of others.

As I have hinted before, some of the greatest love-letters were written and are written, not by famous figures in history and literature, but by people in the lower walks of life. Take, for instance, those penned by Edith Thompson to Frederick Bywaters, just before Bywaters murdered her husband in her presence, and probably with her assistance. She wrote them in 1921–22, when employed as a bookkeeper in a small millinery shop in London. The letters are terribly sincere, and have a real tragic note. Little did Edith Thompson realize, when on the scaffold in Holloway Prison, that these very letters to her accomplice, which helped to convince her, would some day be given to an inquisitive world, edited, with a preface, by Filson Young.

But the great make better copy, so I shall stick to my last!

Of all the love-letters ever written, I think Napoleon's are the least interesting. Unfortunately, some of the early ones to Josephine are lost. They may have contained at least a flicker of the vital spark, but I doubt it. Eight to Josephine were sold in London in 1933, and brought forty-four hundred pounds. In one, dated March 9, 1796, the month of their marriage, Napoleon wrote with unusual passion:

> You must forgive me, my dear friend, the love with which you inspire me has taken away all my reason; I shall never regain it. My presentments are so terrible that I should be contented if I could see you, press you for two hours against my heart and then die together.

But the letters with which we are familiar, the ones to his second wife, Marie Louise, are typical examples of that quiet emotion which, I understand, all wives resent—just plain colorless affection. Nevertheless, more than three hundred letters to Marie Louise were sold at auction recently in London and were bought by the French Government for fifteen thousand pounds.

Napoleon did write one magnificent letter which I eventually acquired, and which is now in the Pierpont Morgan Library. It has nothing to do with his own grand amours, yet it is a tempestuous one, relating to the first great international romance of this country.

Jerome Bonaparte, brother of the First Consul, was only nineteen when he met, loved, and married the beautiful Betsy Patterson in Baltimore. Napoleon, when apprised of the ceremony, which took place on Christmas Eve, 1803, became terribly enraged, and ruthlessly refused to recognize the marriage. In 1805, Jerome, with his wife, left this country for Spain. Napoleon enlisted the help of his mother, the famous Letizia Bonaparte. Napoleon writes her this remarkable letter:

MADAME,

Mr. Jerome Bonaparte has arrived at Lisbon with the woman with whom he is living. I have given orders to this prodigal son to return to Milan, by way of Perpignan, Toulouse, Grenoble, and Turin. I have written him to understand that if he departs from this route he will be arrested. Miss Paterson with whom he lives has taken the precaution of having her brother with her; I have given orders that she be sent back to America. If she withdraws from the orders that I have given and goes to Bordeaux or to Paris, she will be conducted back to Amsterdam, there to be embarked on the first American vessel. I will treat this young man severely, if in the only interview I shall grant him, he shows himself unworthy of the name he bears, if he persists in wishing to continue this liaison, and he is not inclined to wash out the dishonor he has cast upon my name by deserting the flag and his colours for a miserable woman, I will abandon him forever, and perhaps I will make an example [of him] which will prove to young soldiers, to what degree their duty is sacred, and the enormity of the crime which they commit when they desert their flag for a woman. In the supposition that he may return to Milan, write to him, tell him I have been a father to him and that his duty towards me is sacred and that there remains for him, no other salvation but to follow my instructions. Speak to his sister so that she may also write to him, for when I have pronounced sentence I shall be inflexible and his life will be ruined forever.

> Your most affectionate son,
>
> NAPOLEON
> Au Château de Stupinis,
> le 2 floréal an 13—22 April, 1805.

The honors Napoleon promised to bestow upon Jerome, together with the aid of their mother, finally brought the young gentleman around, and by decree of the French Senate, his marriage with the "woman" was annulled. Jerome had evidently none of the backbone of the great Napoleon, or of the determined Letizia, who was a veritable matriarch. Sad to relate, especially in a chapter such as this, Jerome gave up lovely Miss Patterson to marry the plain Princess Catherine of Würtemberg. As a reward, he received the title of

King of Westphalia. I wonder if Jerome, when in the arms of his consort, did not sometimes think of what he had lost, and whether it was worth while to relinquish a great passion for statecraft.

Of all correspondence, love-letters are the first to be destroyed. The fireplace must have consumed many precious examples that collectors would give their very souls to possess. It is this that makes the chase so interesting. Many that have survived are locked up in old libraries. For instance, the epistles—it is a better name for royal letters—of King Henry VIII to Anne Boleyn are in the Vatican.

How I would like to own the love-letters of Casanova; that would be a real triumph. There is a little cache where the original manuscript of the famous *Memoirs* remains, together with hundreds of letters from the charming ladies of his intimate circle. If I reveal the place, I am sure someone will forestall me. Yet I will do so, for I like to ruminate upon the fact that Casanova, after his many amatory adventures, settled down as a librarian in the castle of Count Waldstein, at Dux, in Bohemia, where the celebrated *Memoirs* were written, and where the love-letters now are. There is a rumor, but I cannot vouch for it, that the count considers installing in his ancestral library a cooling system on account of heat generated by the inflammatory content.

Doctor Samuel Johnson and Mrs. Thrale were a strange pair. Reams of paper have been consumed telling of the most celebrated literary friendship of the eighteenth century. It must be said at the start that Johnson was also the friend of her husband. In fact, when Mr. Thrale stood for Parliament the great lexicographer wrote his speeches for him. Johnson was thus one of the early ghost writers. He also helped him in his brewery business, a rare combination. When Mr. Thrale departed this life, his wife, who never really loved him, and frankly declared before her marriage that Thrale only took her because other ladies refused him, became secretly engaged to Gabriel Piozzi, a handsome Italian musician, whom she first met in 1780. The problem was how to inform Doctor Johnson of the event. He had written her many letters revealing his intense regard for her. After all, Johnson had been her dearest friend and mentor. How could she tell the old man, who was then seventy-three, of her new attachment?

She ended by sending him a circular letter! In this she announced her marriage to Piozzi, with a few explanatory remarks written on the back. Doctor Johnson's reply to Mrs. Thrale is exactly what we would expect of him:

> MADAM:
>
> If I interpret your letter right, you are ignomini-ously married, if it is yet undone, let us at once talk together. If you have abandoned your children and your religion, God forgive your wickedness; if you have forfeited your Fame, and your country, may your folly do no further mischief.
>
> If the last act is yet to do, I, who have loved you, esteemed you, reverenced you, and served you, I who long thought you the first of humankind, entreat that before your fate is irrevocable, I may once more see you.
>
> I was, I once was MADAM
> most truly yours,
> SAM. JOHNSON

Fifteen years ago, I set myself a tremendous task which, at first, I never dreamed I could accomplish. I wanted to own the finest collection in the world of "Rabbie" Burns. To my surprise and delight, it proved to be easier than I thought. Mr. Robert B. Adam, of Buffalo, New York, set me off to a flying start by offering his wonderful collection, including such treasures as the original manuscripts of *For a' That and a' That, Tam o' Shanter, Bruce to His*

Men at Bannockburn, and more than fifty others. With these in my possession, I was and am constantly on the lookout, not only for manuscripts but for Burns's letters—love-letters.

Burns never made a secret of his attachment for several ladies—Jean Armour, Mrs. M'Lehose (Clarinda), Mrs. Riddell, and Mrs. Dunlop. He immortalized them, as he did everything he touched. The letters he wrote them are amazing. They appear at auction only at rare intervals and fetch a very substantial sum. I paid eight hundred pounds for one of mine. He exposes his soul in them, and yet, with all the intense passion of his being, they exhibit a nobility of character and a chivalrous bearing that were inherent in him. Even in affairs of the heart, Burns was outspoken and fearless. There was nothing of the "professional" lover in them so frequently found in the amatory correspondence of Lord Byron. I have many of the letters that Burns wrote his fair admirers, but give extracts from only two.

On December 13, 1789, he wrote Mrs. Dunlop concerning his hopes and fears of the future life:

> Can it be possible that when I resign this frail, feverish being, I shall still find myself in conscious existence! When the last gasp of agony has announced that I am no more to those that knew me & the few who loved me; when the cold, stiffened, unconscious ghastly corse is resigned into earth, to be the prey of unsightly reptiles & to become in time a trodden clod, shall I yet be warm in life, seeing & seen, enjoying & enjoyed?

To Mrs. M'Lehose, the celebrated Clarinda, Burns wrote in a lighter vein under the fanciful name of Sylvander:

> I shall certainly be ashamed of thus scrawling whole sheets of incoherence.—The only unity, (a sad word

with Poet's and Critics!) in my ideas, is Clarinda. There my heart "reigns and revels."

What art thou Love! Whence are those charms,
　　That dost thou bear'st an universal rule!
For thee the soldier quits his arms,
　　The king turns slave, the wise man fool.
In vain we chase thee from the field,
　　And with cool thoughts resist thy yoke:
Next tide of blood, Alas! we yield;
　　And all those high resolves are broke!

SYLVANDER

Burns became adept at writing love-letters and was so proud of his ability that he frequently wrote them for his friends. The following letter, entirely in his handwriting, is from the original in the possession of that enthusiastic and unregenerate book-lover, my dear friend Mr. Frank J. Hogan:

MADAM

What excuse to make for the liberty I am going to assume in this letter, I am utterly at a loss.—I—have the most unfeigned respect for your accomplished worth, if the most ardent attachment, if sincerity & truth—if these on my part will in any degree weigh with you, my apology is these & these alone.—Little as have had the pleasure of your acquaintance, it has been enough to convince me what invaluable happiness must be his, whom you shall honor with your particular regard, & and more than enough to inform me how unworthy I am to offer myself a candidate for that partiality. In this kind of trembling hope,

Madam, I intend very soon doing myself the honor
of waiting on you; persuaded that however little Miss
Gordon may be disposed to attend to the suit of a
lover so unworthy of her as I am, she is still too good
to despise an honest man whose only fault, as to her, is
loving her too much for his own peace.

I have the honor to be MADAM
your most devoted humble servant.
Dumfries, March 22, 1785.

The love of Shelley for Mary Godwin has been called everything under the sun. Some say it was ideal; others sordid. Whatever
the opinion, it is without doubt one of the great love adventures
in literary annals. In 1814, Shelley, after a lurid courtship, decided
to throw caution to the winds and ran away with Mary. I had to
buy a whole library to obtain the letter Mary wrote to Shelley a
few hours before their elopement. Alas! I regret that I have it no
longer:

MY OWN LOVE:
I do not know by what compulsion I am to answer
you, but your porter says I must, so I do. By a mira-
cle I saved your five pounds & I will bring it. I hope,
indeed, oh my loved Shelley, we shall indeed be happy.
I meet you at three and bring heaps of Skinner street
news. Heaven bless my love and take care of him!

HIS OWN MARY

The elopement caused a veritable sensation. Mary's father,
William Godwin, an improvident bookseller who had written
a treatise on free love, was heartbroken that his own daughter
should have deceived him. To add to his misery, he owed Shelley
money. There is no doubt the alliance spelled tragedy in his mind.

His advocacy of free love must have been to him a bitter pill. In the following letter to his friend John Taylor, Godwin graphically described his wrought-up feelings:

Skinner Street, Aug. 27, 1814

Dear Sir:

I have a story to tell you of the deepest melancholy....You are already acquainted with the name of Shelley, the gentleman who more than twelve months ago undertook by his own assistance to rescue me from my pecuniary difficulties. Not to keep you longer in suspense, he, a married man, has run away with my daughter. I cannot conceive of an event of more accumulated horror.

He lodged at an Inn in Fleet Street and took his meals with me. I had the utmost confidence in him; I knew him susceptible of the noblest sentiments; he was a married man, who had lived happily with his wife for three years. Accordingly the first week of his visit passed in perfect innocence;...On Sunday, June 26th, he accompanied Mary, and her sister Jane Clairmont, to the tomb of Mary's Mother, one mile distant from London; and there, it seems, the impious idea first occurred to him of seducing her, playing the traitor to me and deserting his wife. On Wednesday, the 6th of July, the transaction of the loan was completed; and on the evening of that very day he had the madness to disclose his plans to me, and to ask my consent. I expostulated with him with all the energy of which I was master, and with so much effect that for the moment he promised to give up his licentious love, and return to virtue. I applied all my diligence to waken up a sense of honor and natural affection in the mind of Mary, and I seemed to have succeeded. They both deceived me. In the night of the 27th Mary and her sister Jane escaped from my house; and the next morning when I rose, I found a letter on my dressing table, informing me what they had done.

Shelley's own interpretation of love is embodied in this letter to Mary, written in December 1816, at the sober age of twenty-four:

The gratification of the senses soon becomes a very small part of that profound and complicated senti-ment which we call love. Love, on the contrary, is a universal thirst for a communion, not merely of the senses, but of our whole nature, intellectual, imagina-tive, and sensitive. He who finds his autotype enjoys a love perfect and enduring. If men were properly edu-cated and their natures fully developed, the discovery of the autotype would be easy...

In 1826 there appeared in London a serial issued in twenty parts. The work of a hitherto unknown author, a young law reporter, Charles Dickens, it took the world by storm. It was the case of the man who "awoke one morning and found himself famous." This year, 1936, has seen the hundredth anniversary of the publication of the *Pickwick Papers.* Celebrations in honor of the event have been held in England and in this country by devoted Dickens enthusiasts.

One of the most precious things I have is a portion of the man-uscript of the *Pickwick Papers,* the most valuable Dickens holograph in the world. I recently gave $37,500 to add only five more pages to it. But, of course, this has nothing to do with Dickens's affairs of the heart, except that just before he wrote *Pickwick,* and preceding his unfortunate marriage to Miss Hogarth, he was in love with Miss Maria Beadnell. It seems Miss Beadnell refused the proposals of Charles Dickens because Henry Winter, an energetic young tradesman, had brighter prospects. I wonder if in after years she regretted it. The world knew—and, of course, this included Mrs. Winter—that Dickens was never happy in his married life. Perhaps she thanked her lucky stars she had rejected him. Who knows?

A true account of Thackeray's love for Mrs. Brookfield has yet to be written, as many of the letters he wrote to her are unpublished. A few have been given to the world, but the real ones, written between 1847 and 1853, in which Thackeray freely unburdens his heart, were in the library of my old friend, Mr. A. Conger Goodyear, of Buffalo, New York, safe from the prying eyes of biographers. In 1927, Mr. Goodyear decided to sell them at auction in New York, together with Thackeray's correspondence with Miss Perry and her sister, Mrs. Elliott, to whom he tells many facts of his romance that he did not dare reveal to Mrs. Brookfield. These precious memorials of a great and unselfish love I had to have at all costs, and I did not consider it too much when I paid $29,500. They are now in my book vault in New York. To me, they are far more interesting, more poignant than the letters written by the Brownings. A hopeless love, like Thackeray's for Mrs. Brookfield, is far more dramatic; one moment he is in the clouds, the next fallen to the bitter earth.

Thackeray made no effort to hide his friendship for Mrs. Brookfield, and in 1847 he wrote to her:

> But thank God I have never concealed the affection I have for you; your husband knows it as well as you or I do, and I think I have such a claim to the love of both of you as no relationship, however close, ought to question or supersede....As for William [Mr. Brookfield], I am bound to him by benefits by the most generous

confidence and repeated proofs of friendship, and to you dear lady by an affection which I hope won't finish with my life of which you have formed for a long time past one of the greatest and I hope the purest pleasures. If I had a bad thought towards you I think I could not look my friend or you in the face, and I see no shame in owning that I love you. I have Wm.'s permission, your's, that of my own heart and conscience for constantly, daily if I can, seeing you. Who has a right to forbid me my greatest happiness.

Again Thackeray wrote to the lady of his heart:

We will love each other while we may here and afterwards if you go first you will kneel for me in heaven and bring me there—if I, I swear the best thought is to remember that I shall have your love surviving me and with a constant tenderness blessing my memory. I can't all perish living in your heart. That in itself is a sort of seal and assurance of heaven....Say that I die and live yet in the love of my survivors, isn't that a warrant of immortality almost? Say that my 2 dearest friends precede me and enter into God's futurity spotless and angelical I feel that I have 2 advocates in Heaven & that my love penetrates there as it were. It seems to me that Love proves God. By love I believe and am saved.

Many of the letters to Mrs. Brookfield were written when Thackeray was on a lecture tour in America. They contain not only expressions of his love but bits of news. He thus writes to her: "The prettiest girl in Philadelphia, poor soul, has read *Vanity Fair* twelve times." I wonder who she was!

Although at first Thackeray states that he was devoted to the husband, William Brookfield, I believe that later the friendship waned. Thackeray, as was natural, really began to hate him. The following extract from one of Thackeray's letters in the Perry-Elliott correspondence is proof. He thus writes to Miss Perry near the close of the romance:

> God bless her. For all the pain and grief to both of us: I would not have *not* had her love for anything in the world. It's apart from desire, or jealousy of any one else, that I think of her and shall always. There is nothing I know of have ever read or thought of so lovely as her nature is; the dark spirit is on her poor husband still I fear. He was not fit to be the mate of such an angelical creature as that; what a constant loneliness and grief and rage his life must be—poor old fellow; it is he who is the most unhappy of us three.

Love-Letters of Famous Americans! What a title for a book. In colonial days, before the Revolution, writers seldom preserved such dangerous correspondence, and the love-letters of Washington, Jefferson, Madison, John Adams, and Alexander Hamilton are rarely met with. It is said that Martha Washington, shortly before her death, destroyed nearly all the letters addressed to her by George. A wise woman. How many secrets have been revealed when packets of old love-letters, carefully preserved, and tied with the proverbial blue ribbon, are discovered and published for the delectation of a naughty world.

"I profess myself a votary to love," Washington writes in 1758 to Miss Fairfax. He was a surveyor on his own estate in Virginia, and had many kind neighbors, no doubt. He often went to Alexandria and Williamsburg on little trips to visit the ladies of his acquaintance. It is a pity we do not know more of Washington's early love adventures. When he finally became engaged to Mrs. Martha Custis, a charming, rich widow, he gave up all thought of anyone but her, as the following extract from a letter, unusually frank for him, written when he was about thirty-three years old, proves:

> DEAR FRIEND ROBIN:
>
> [...] my Place of Residence is at present His Lordship's where I might was my heart disengaged pass my time very pleasantly as there is a very agreeable Young Lady lives in the same house [Colonel George Fairfax's wife's sister] but as that's only adding Fuel to fire it makes me the more uneasy for by often and unavoidably being in Company with her revives my former Passion for your Low Land Beauty where as was I to live more retired from young women I might in some measure eliviate my sorrows by burying that chast and troublesome Passion in the grave of oblivion of eternall forgetfulness for as I am very well assured that's the only antidote or remedy that I ever shall be relieved by or only recess that can administer any cure or help to me as I am well convinced was I every to attempt anything I should only get a denial which would be only adding grief to uneasiness.

In view of the extreme rarity of letters of George to Martha, I give here one of the few now extant:

July 20, 1758

> To MRS. MARTHA CUSTIS:
>
> We have begun our march for the Ohio. A courier

is starting for Williamsburg, and I embrace the opportunity to send a few words to one whose life is now inseparable from mine. Since that happy hour when we made our pledges to each other, my thoughts have been continually going to you as another Self. That an all-powerful Providence may keep us both in safety is the prayer of your ever faithful and affectionate friend.

Living not far from George Washington in Virginia was young Thomas Jefferson. I always wanted a love-letter of Jefferson's, or one relating to his love affairs. I waited patiently twenty years. Finally, two came up for sale, together with the greatest letter ever written by Jefferson. It was the famous penned in Philadelphia on July first, with a postscript written July 2, 1776. In it he states: "If any doubt has arisen as to me, my country will have my political creed in the form of a 'Declaration' which I was lately directed to draw." What a thrilling letter for Americans to read! This and the two early amatory ones were written to William Fleming, a member of the Committee of the Virginia Convention.

Unable, on November 20, 1930, to attend the sale myself, I sent my assistant, a namesake of the owner, John Fleming. I gave him an unlimited bid on the letters, telling him to phone me the result. "And be sure to get the ones about the Virginia ladies," was my final admonition.

A few hours later he was breathless on the wire. "I bought the Jefferson Declaration letter," he said, "for twenty-three thousand dollars!"

"Cheap," I replied. "It is a great letter! How about the others?"

"I bought them at a price that will please you." And it did.

These letters reveal Jefferson as a rollicking young fellow with a roving eye. Here is an extract from one written when he was twenty-one years old:

Richmond [October, 1763]

DEAR WILL:

Last Saturday I left Ned Carters where I had been happy in other good company, but particularly that of Miss Jenny Taliaferro: and though I can view the beauties of this world with the most philosophical indifference, I could not but be sensible of the justice of the character you had given me of her. She has in my opinion a great resemblance of Nancy Wilton, but prettier. I was vastly pleased with her playing on the spinette and singing, I could not help to calling to mind those sublime verses of the Cumberland genius

Oh, how I was charmed to be
Orpheus music all in thee

when you see Patsy Dandridge tell her "god bless her," I do not like the ups and downs of a country life: today you are frolicking with a fine girl and tomorrow you are moping by yourself. Thank god! I shall shortly be where my happiness will be less interrupted. I shall salute all the girls below in your name, particularly S-y P-r. Dear Will I have thought of the cleverest plan of life that can be imagined. You exchange your land for Edgehill or I mine for Fairfields. You marry S-y P-r, I marry R-a B-l and get a pole chair and a pair of keen horses, practice the law in the same courts, and drive about to all the dances in the country together....I am dear Will

Yours affectionately,
TH. JEFFERSON

The letters Benjamin Franklin wrote his wife, Deborah, from the moment he met her until her death in 1774 are among his most charming. He always relates little bits of news, amusing anecdotes of the great people he met in France and England during his many visits. Most of the letters to Deborah are in the library of the American Philosophical Society in Philadelphia.

Franklin wrote one letter which some think should have been burnt, but which has been miraculously preserved for the delight of posterity. It is his celebrated letter written on June 25, 1745, concerning "Wives and Old Mistresses." The original manuscript came to me in a most curious way. When the Library of Congress obtained the Franklin Papers from Henry Stevens in 1882, the letter was strangely missing. Perhaps Stevens "held it out" thinking it was too good a thing to entrust to the American public, and he was quite right! Stevens finally sold it to a gentleman in Chicago who left it in his will to an institution in that chaste city. Chicago, being known for its purity, and not tolerating anything even slightly indelicate, offered it to me—at a price, of course, for it did not hesitate to profit, like a frail sister, from its shame. I do not give it here, as in this enlightened age, it has been frequently reprinted.

I once owned a very spirited letter of Franklin's to a charming young lady, of austere New England, Miss Kitty Ray.

> DEAR KATY,
>
> I left New England slowly & with great Reluctance. Short Days Journeys, and loitering Visits on the Road, for three or four Weeks, manifested my Unwillingness to quit a Country in which I drew my first Breath, spent my earliest & most Pleasant Days, and had now received so many fresh Marks of the People's Goodness and Benevolence, in the kind & affectionate Treatment I had everywhere met with. I almost

forgot I had a home; till I was more than halfway towards it; till I had, one by one, parted with all my New England Friends, and was got into the western Borders of Connecticut among meer Strangers: then, like an old Man, who having buried all he lov'd in this World, begins to think of Heaven, I begun to think of & wish for Home; and as I drew nearer, I found the Attraction stronger and stronger, my Diligence and Speed increas'd with my Impatience, I drove on violently, and made such long stretches at that a very few Days brought me to my own House, and to the Arms of my good old Wife and Children, where I remain, Thanks to God, at present well and happy.

Persons subject to the Hyp, complain of the North East Wind as increasing their Malady. But since you promis'd to send me Kisses in the Wind, and I find you as good as your Word, 'tis to me the gayest Wind that blows and gives me the best Spirits. I write this during a N. East Storm of Snow, the greatest we have had this Winter; your Favours come mix'd with the Snowy Fleeces, which are pure as your Virgin Innocence, white as your lovely Bosom—and as cold.

When Franklin arrived in France in 1777 as an emissary of the new republic, he met many charming and distinguished women. He wrote, during his mission to Paris, to his sister Jane Mecom: "I hope, however, to preserve the regard you mention of the French ladies, for their society and conversation, when I have time to enjoy it, is extremely agreeable."

One of the chief objects of his visit was to secure a loan from France, which was absolutely necessary if the war with England was to continue. Franklin made several attempts to obtain a grant from the King, without success. He could make no headway with Monsieur Brillon, one of the King's financial advisers. He was at his wits' end. Suddenly a thought came to him, for which is rightly called our greatest diplomat. He determined to approach Monsieur Brillon through his wife, a beautiful and affectionate woman. When they first met, Franklin was seventy-five; she thirty-six. He was instantly attracted to her. He spoke feelingly of the distress of the struggling colonies, and that if help should not soon be obtained, the war would be lost. Needless to say, it worked like a charm. I purchased, not long ago, the actual receipt given by Franklin to the Treasurer of France for five hundred thousand livres; one of the earliest, if not the earliest, foreign loans made to the United States.

Franklin wrote many extravagant and witty letters from his delightful little house in Passy to his charming neighbor, Madame Brillon. Sometimes he enclosed with them little compositions, such as the "Story of a Whistle," which is now a classic. They all contained bits of wisdom in the inimitable manner of Poor Richard. Franklin was proud of them himself. Where were the originals of these exquisite letters to Madame Brillon? I did not know. I had seen copies of some of them, but the whereabouts of the originals was a puzzle. Some years ago, Bernard Fay was engaged in writing his life of Franklin. I wrote to him and received no answers. One day he turned up at my office in New York. Yes, he knew. He had discovered them. In an old château in France, in the possession of one of the descendants of Madame Brillon. Through the good offices of M. Fay, I finally obtained them. The letters were in beautiful condition, having no doubt been kept with the tenderest care by the lady to whom they were sent.

"Yes, my dear child," writes Franklin to Madame Brillon, "I love you as a father, with all my heart. It is true I occasionally suspect my heart of wishing to go farther, but I try to hide that from myself."

I regret I have space to give only the famous Treaty Letter, written while Franklin was engaged in his great work of drafting the Definitive Treaty between the United States and Great Britain, France and Spain. It is dated from Passy, July 27 (1783):

To Madame Brillon:

What a difference, my dear Friend, between you and me! You find my faults so many as to be innumerable, which I can see but one in you; and perhaps that is the fault of my spectacles. The fault I mean is that of covetousness, by which you would engross all my affection, and permit me none for the other amiable ladies of your country. You seem to imagine that it cannot be divided without being diminish'd. In which you mistake the nature of the thing and forget the situation in which you have plac'd and hold me. You renounce and exclude arbitrarily everything corporal from our Amour, except such a merely civil embrace now and then you permit to a country cousin...

You see by this time how unjust you are in your demands, and in the open war you declare against me if I do not comply with them. Indeed it is I that have the most reason to complain. My poor little boy, whom you ought methinks to have cherish'd instead of being fat and jolly like those in your elegant Drawings, is meagre and starv'd almost to death for want of the substantial nourishment which you his mother inhumanely deny him, and yet would now clip his little wings to prevent his seeking it elsewhere!

I fancy we shall neither of us get anything by this war, and therefore as feeling myself the weakest, I will do what indeed ought always to be done by the wisest, be first in making the propositions for peace. That a peace may be lasting, the Articles of the Treaty should be regulated upon the Principles of the most perfect Equity and Reciprocity. In this view I have drawn up & offer the following viz:

Article I.
There shall be eternal Peace, Friendship & Love, between Madame B. and Mr. F.

Article 2.
In order to maintain the same inviolably Made. B. on her part stipulates and agrees, that Mr. F. shall come to her whenever she sends for him.

Article 3.
That he shall stay with her as long as she pleases.

Article 4.
That when he is with her, he shall be oblig'd to drink tea, play Chess, hear Musick, or do any other thing that she requires of him.

Article 5.
And that he shall love no other woman but herself.

Article 6.
And that said Mr. F. on his part stipulates and agrees that he will go away from Madame B.'s whenever he pleases.

Article 7.
That he will stay away as long as he pleases.

Article 8.
That when he is with her he will do what he pleases.

Article 9.
And that he will love any other woman so far as he finds her amiable.

Let me know what you think of these Preliminaries.

To me they seem to express the true meaning and Intention of each party more plainly than most treaties. I shall insist pretty strongly on the eighth Article, tho' I despair of ever finding any other woman that I could love with equal tenderness; being ever, my dear dear friend

Yours most sincerely,

B. F.

Love-letters of Abraham Lincoln are practically unobtainable. To find an authentic one is a real achievement. Because there are so few, the clever forger has taken advantage of our common frailty, supplying enthusiastic but gullible collectors with ardent Lincoln letters addressed to his early loves, Ann Rutledge and Mary Owens. People are constantly bringing me their "Lincoln" letters, and it is incredible how many persons who should know better are taken in. The letters are time-stained, for forgers can age paper as quickly as distillers can age their spirits. Experts, too, have been fooled. But here is a real one. Not exactly a passionate love-letter but a romantic one, a mock petition, written in a facetious mood from Springfield in 1839, when he was thirty. It is signed by Lincoln and three of his friends, and addressed to Mrs. Orville Browning. It runs:

To THE HONORABLE MRS. BROWNING:

We, the undersigned, respectfully represent to your Honoress, that we are in great need of your society in the town of Springfield and therefore humbly pray that your Honoress will repair forthwith to the seat of Government bringing in your train all ladies in general who may be at your command and all Mrs. Browning's sisters in particular and as faithful and dutiful petitioners we promise that if you grant this our request, we will render unto your Honoress due attention and faithful obedience to your orders in general and to Miss Browning's in particular.

In tender consideration whereof we pray your Honoress to grant your humble petitioners their above request and such other and further relief in the premises as to your Honoress may seem right and proper; and your petitioners as in duty bound will ever pray, etc.

(Signed)   LINCOLN

O. B. WEBB

J. J. HARDIN

JOHN DAWSON

Lincoln's love—if you care to call it that—for Mary Owens began in 1836. She must have been, from the brief accounts we have of her, an attractive, intelligent woman. Lincoln deeply admired her, and in a short time proposed. He wrote her some of the strangest love-letters ever penned by man. They are filled with local political gossip and reasons why she should not marry him! Reading between the lines, one comes to the conclusion that in them Lincoln tried to be scrupulously honest and fair, even to sacrificing his own happiness for the woman to whom he was so devoted. Lincoln knew he was no Adonis, and he knew also that he could never endow her with worldly goods. He states so plainly in his letter—too plainly. According to the Lover's Code, 600th Revised Edition, Article 987, Chapter XXIV, Page 9911, which he evidently never studied, the mistake Lincoln made was to put his shortcomings into print. He was his own devil's advocate—a dangerous thing in wooing. After reading the following letter, written by Lincoln to Miss Owens from Springfield on May 7, 1837, you can hardly blame the fair recipient for not encouraging the young lawyer's attentions. Perhaps she could not read between the lines:

FRIEND MARY:

I am often thinking of what we said about your coming to live at Springfield. I am afraid you would not be satisfied. There is a great deal of flourishing about in carriages here, which it would be your doom to see without sharing it. You would have to be poor, without the means of hiding your poverty. Do you believe you could bear that patiently? Whatever woman may cast her lot with mine, should any ever do so, it is my intention to do all in my power to make her happy and contented; and there is nothing I can imagine that would make me more unhappy than to fail in the effort. I know I should be much happier with you that the way I am, provided I saw no signs of discontent in you. What you have said to me may have been in the way of jest, or I may have misunderstood it. If so, then let it be forgotten; if otherwise, I much wish you would think seriously before you decide. What I have said I will most positively abide by, provided you wish it. My opinion is that you have better not do it. You have not been accustomed to hardship, and it may be more severe than you can now imagine. I know you are capable of thinking correctly on any subject, and if you deliberate maturely upon this before you decide, then I am willing to abide your decision.

What Lincoln evidently needed was a lover's lexicon.

Not everyone in the colonies, like Franklin and Jefferson, could spontaneously put his emotions onto paper. Thousands had to rely on the poetic fancies of others.

In the early days in America, almost every bookseller had on his shelves what were called "Ready Letter Writers." The printing presses turned them out by thousands. They contained letters on every conceivable subject, and for every occasion. All you have to do was to copy one that pleased you and send it over your own signature. I inherited one of these quaint compendiums, which was issued in Philadelphia in 1793:

THE AMERICAN LETTER-WRITER:

CONTAINING, A VARIETY OF LETTERS ON THE MOST COMMON OCCASIONS IN LIFE, VIZ: FRIENDSHIP, DUTY, ADVICE, BUSINESS, AMUSEMENT, LOVE, MARRIAGE, COURTSHIP, &C....TO WHICH ARE PREFIXED, DIRECTIONS FOR WRITING LETTERS, AND THE PROPER FORMS OF ADDRESS.

Judging from the timeworn covers, it must have been frequently used by members of my family.

These little books are still published, and booksellers tell me they have a ready sale. This reminds me of an interesting story.

Some years ago I had the pleasure of meeting a lady of unusual grace and brilliancy. She was a book-collector. To me, that was her greatest charm. One day I showed her my little volume on the art of letter-writing. Instantly her usual calm expression changed and her eyes took on a startled look.

"Of all the women in the world," she said, "why did you bring it to me?"

She then told me her story.

"I was eighteen years old," she said, "when a young man for whom I did not particularly care asked me to marry him. He kept repeating his proposal; my parents were on his side, for he was energetic and ambitious. I, however, did not love him, and constantly refused his offers. One morning I received a letter. I knew the handwriting, and reluctantly opened it. It was one of the most beautiful letters I had ever read, filled with tender sentiment and the most impassioned expressions of his love. There was so much fire in it, so much burning desire that the letter seemed to scorch my fingers. Yet I wondered how a man of his cold exterior could have written such a letter. Had I misjudged him? I showed the letter to my parents—girls did that in the nineties—and they assured me that only a fellow of exceptional worth could write like that. So, I married him.

"We lived together for nearly twenty years. One day, looking through an old trunk, I found a worn book with a slip of paper marking a page. I opened it and had the shock of my life.

"Of course, you know the rest of the story! That letter, so tender and passionate, the letter that had caused me to marry him, my husband had copied out of that very volume. I had discovered it years too late. As I come of a generation that considers a contract a contract, I could not walk out of my husband's life because of a counterfeit love-letter. My advice to you is," she said in parting,

"never keep an old love-letter; it may prove a boomerang."
"Better still," I rejoined, "never write one."
In the language of the poet:

> Lives of great men all remind us,
> As these pages o'er we turn,
> That we're apt to leave behind us
> Letters that we ought to burn.

OSCAR WILDE: BIOGRAPHICAL TIMELINE

1854   Born in Dublin, Ireland, one of two children of Sir William Wilde, a physician and writer, and Jane Francesca Elgee Wilde, called Speranza, a writer.

1864   Enters Portora Royal School at Enniskillen.

1871   Enrolls at Trinity College, Dublin.

1874–79 Attends Magdalen College, Oxford.

1878   Awarded Newdigate Prize at Oxford for his poem *Ravenna*.

1881   Publishes a first volume of verse, *Poems*.

1882   Goes on a lecture tour of the United States and Canada to showcase his aesthetic worldview, where his rhetorical abilities and wit prove popular.

1883   His first play *Vera; Or the Nihilists* is produced in New York City.

1884   Marries Constance Lloyd, daughter of a Dublin barrister. The Wildes live in Chelsea, an artistic area of London. Goes on a lecture tour of Britain and Ireland to talk about aesthetics.

1887–89 Works as the editor of *Woman's World*.

1888   Publishes *The Happy Prince and Other Tales*, a collection of original fairy tales that contain themes addressed also in later works.

1889   Publishes an essay on Shakespeare's sonnets in *Blackwood's Magazine*, "The Portrait of Mr. W. H." The essay argues that many of Shakespeare's sonnets are addressed to a man.

1890   Publishes a serialized version of *The Picture of Dorian Gray* in *Lippincott's Magazine*, whose editors excise several homoerotic passages they fear to be controversial.

1891   Publishes the essay collection, *Intentions*, which outlines some of Wilde's aesthetic philosophy; *Lord Arthur Savile's Crime and Other Stories*, a collection of short stories; and his only novel, *The Picture of Dorian Gray*. The novel is met with controversy over its alleged immorality and the claim that art must not be judged according to moral standards. Publishes another collection of stories, *A House of Pomegranates*. First meeting and beginning of Wilde's friendship with the Oxford student Lord Alfred Douglas, nicknamed "Bosie" by his mother. Writes *Salomé* in French, which is not produced in London due to a law forbidding theatrical depiction of biblical characters.

1892   *Lady Windermere's Fan* premieres in London to great success.

1893   *A Woman of No Importance* premieres to great success in London. Publishes *Lady Windermere's Fan* and *Salomé* in French.

1894   Writes another play, *The Importance of Being Earnest*.

1895   *An Ideal Husband* premieres at the Haymarket Theatre and *The Importance of Being Earnest* at the St. James's Theatre to great acclaim by audiences and critics. Wilde and Lord Douglas flaunt their relationship in public, provoking Douglas's father to threaten Wilde and to accuse him of being a homosexual. Wilde sues for libel, but after he dominates part of the trial with his witty replies, he abandons the case when incriminating evidence of paid affairs with younger men is made public in cross-examination. Wilde has a few hours after the first trial is suspended to leave London for Paris but decides to wait for his arrest. In two more trials that are reported by the press around the globe, he is found guilty of "gross indecency" with men and sentenced to two years at hard labor. He is bankrupted and publicly humiliated, with many friends, business associates and others turning on him. A few supporters remain.

1896   *Salomé* is performed in Paris while Wilde is in prison in England.

1897   In prison he writes *De Profundis*, an autobiographical letter addressed to Lord Douglas published in part in 1905 that also chronicles a turn to religion. Upon his release from prison, he goes into exile in France with the help of a few loyal friends, where he lives under an alias, Sebastian Melmoth. His wife has changed her name and left England with their two sons; Wilde will not see her or his sons again.

1898   He publishes his best-known poem, "The Ballad of Reading Gaol," set in prison, and two letters on prison reform. Against his friends' advice and despite legal agreements to stop all contact with Lord Douglas, Wilde moves to Naples with Bosie until the latter is forced by his family to leave. Lady Douglas financially supports Wilde for a while during this time, as do other friends. He tries to revive his writing career especially in the United States. He never apologizes for the relationships that put him in jail. His wife dies.

1900   After being baptized as a Catholic, he dies penniless of cerebral meningitis at the Hôtel D'Alsace in Paris and is buried at Bagneux Cemetery, then at the outskirts of Paris.

In 1909, Wilde's remains are transferred at the expense of friends and under the supervision of a friend and Wilde's son, Vyvyan, who becomes his literary executor, to the Père Lachaise cemetery in Paris where his tomb is a site of pilgrimage today.

www.ingramcontent.com/pod-product-compliance
Lightning Source LLC
Chambersburg PA
CBHW030349180626
46812CB00007B/2815